Rei Rei is a teacher, astrologer, and writer from Liverpool in the United Kingdom. After a mystical experience that transformed his life for the better over a decade ago, he is dedicated to doing his part in creating a more coherent and compassionate society.

I dedicate this version to my parents, without them, this book would not exist and nor would I.

Thank you for everything you do, not only for me, but for the rest of our family.

This book is *not* designed to replace any kind of professional care, medication, or therapy you may have been prescribed. If you find yourself struggling or overwhelmed, seek professional care immediately.

It is okay, *not* be to okay.

Rei Rei

THE LABYRINTH: REWIRING THE NODES IN THE MAZE OF YOUR MIND
(Rewired Edition)

AUSTIN MACAULEY PUBLISHERS™
LONDON • CAMBRIDGE • NEW YORK • SHARJAH

Copyright © Rei Rei (2021)

The right of Rei Rei to be identified as author of this work has been asserted by the author in accordance with section 77 and 78 of the Copyright, Designs and Patents Act 1988.

All rights reserved. No part of this publication may be reproduced, stored in a retrieval system, or transmitted in any form or by any means, electronic, mechanical, photocopying, recording, or otherwise, without the prior permission of the publishers.

Any person who commits any unauthorised act in relation to this publication may be liable to criminal prosecution and civil claims for damages.

A CIP catalogue record for this title is available from the British Library.

ISBN 9781398425491 (Paperback)
ISBN 9781398425507 (Hardback)
ISBN 9781398425514 (ePub e-book)

www.austinmacauley.com

First Published (2021)
Austin Macauley Publishers Ltd
25 Canada Square
Canary Wharf
London
E14 5LQ

Thank you for everyone who has supported me over the years and especially Austin Macauley Publishers, for allowing this revised version of my book.

Let's *be* the future, together.

Table of Contents

Introduction	11
The Meditative Life	15
Abundance	18
Affirmations	22
Anger	26
Anxiety	29
Appreciation	32
Assumptions	34
Awakening	38
Beliefs	40
The Rules of the Game	42
Making the Unconscious, Conscious	44
Core Beliefs	46
Challenges	49
Choice	52
Christ/Krishna Consciousness	56
Compassion	62
Conditioning	66
Confusion	69
Contrast	72
Criticism	76
Crying	79
Desire	81
Destiny	85
Disassociation	87
Ego	90
Emotions	95
Expectations	100
Forgiveness	103
Getting Creative: Building A Future Self	106
God	112
Grounding	118

Guilt and Shame	121
Habits	125
Heaven and Hell	130
Imagination	134
Intimacy	138
Karma	141
Knowledge and Wisdom	144
Loneliness	148
Love	151
Manifesting	155
Marriage	160
Maturity	163
Meditation	166
Mind	173
Money	178
Motivations	182
Nonattachment	185
Playfulness	189
Power	193
Process	197
Relationships	201
Religion	204
Renunciation	208
Resilience	211
Self-Hate	214
Space	217
Stillness	220
Synchronicity	223
The Unknown	226
Validation	229
Yoga	232
Conclusion	237
Contact	241

INTRODUCTION

The Labyrinth: Rewiring the Nodes in the Maze of your Mind is not a book you read from cover to cover; it is one you keep with you at all times. Whenever you're triggered into an undesirable state, flick to the section relevant to what the present moment contains. This guide is nonlinear, which means you can jump in at any part you prefer, and I hope it benefits you throughout your awakening process.

I'll be covering various metaphysical concepts that are generally misunderstood by society. There are two ways to define an idea: in an expansive or limiting way. In this book, I'll be redefining these concepts so they can prove beneficial to your development. Changing your perspective of these truths will enable you to not only experience them but also dissolve the limitations you *believe* the illusions of the past have inflicted upon you.

Most people conform to a fear-based worldview; they've bought into a plethora of beliefs that unconsciously dictate their lives. These unconscious perceptions convince them to perpetuate behaviours that don't serve them because everyone around them is doing the same; monkey see, monkey do.

For the most part, society is a mixed bag. We adopt positive core values and beliefs from those around us, but also a host of disempowering mindsets that are unconsciously passed down from generation to generation. Adhering to society's *limiting* beliefs creates a bitter, resentful attitude toward life and living in such a state attracts negativity. When people identify solely with a persona that is moulded by past experiences, they lose touch with their timeless self.

The good news is that we *can* change our state of being any time, but most only decide to when the proverbial monkey throws a wrench at them. It usually requires a dreadful experience to convince a person change is necessary; in this book, however, I aim to help people bring their limiting beliefs into consciousness, empowering them to change without needing to hit rock bottom.

It is a scientific fact that between the ages zero to six, children are significantly more receptive to their surroundings than during adulthood. Their brain is locked in *theta* brain waves, which are akin to a recording device. They absorb beliefs, behaviours, and mimic other's reactions merely by observing them. Children have what is known by neuroscientists as mirror-neurons, which means their brain is wired in such a way that they copy everything they experience in their outer environment. As a result, their family, friends, schoolteachers, and pretty much everyone in their society, has contributed, in some way, to conditioning them to fit in with their culture.

"A third story concerns the plasticity of the youthful mind. I heard my mother remark occasionally: 'A man who accepts a job under anyone is a slave.' That impression became so indelibly fixed that even after my marriage I refused all positions. I met expenses by investing my family endowment in land. Moral: Good and positive suggestions should instruct the sensitive ears of children. Their early ideas long remain sharply etched."
– Sri Yukteswar (Autobiography of a Yogi)

No one is to blame; this book isn't about pointing the finger at others, as you chose your society before incarnating in physical reality. The limitations you've inherited are the challenges you've agreed to overcome in this life. You've come to this world to play the game of self-discovery, to unveil your true self amidst a plethora of darkness, limitations, and illusions. Physical incarnations are self-imposed on a level of consciousness your thinking mind cannot fathom; acceptance of this truth, however, can work wonders.

Repetition programmes the subconscious mind. You don't have to think about how to open the refrigerator door, for example, as you've done it so many times that it's become *automatic*. The subconscious is the habit mind, which isn't a bad thing in and of itself. It also contains a host of mental and emotional patterns, that have a considerable impact, not only your behaviour but also the kind of people and situations you attract in your life. The reprogramming of the subconscious becomes a challenge, however, when a person develops a whirlwind of patterns that sabotage their experience of life. This book aims to help them break free of these automatic processes.

"Our thoughts are mainly controlled by our subconscious, which is largely formed before the age of six, and you cannot change the subconscious mind by just thinking about it. That's why the power of positive thinking will not work for most people. The subconscious mind is like a tape player. Until you change the tape, it will not change."

– Dr Bruce H, Lipton PhD

Emotions *reflect* your perception of the environment; it is fundamentally your beliefs that must be changed if you wish to start perceiving differently.

I don't expect you to agree with everything in this book, as life is a matter of perspective; we all see some things differently, and that's all well and good. What you do agree with, however, I want you to memorise to such an extent, that you don't need to pick up the book to apply the information to the circumstance at hand.

For example, a situation triggers you into depression, sadness, or anger; instead of wallowing in the emotion, respond with awareness as all triggers are opportunities for the expansion of your consciousness. Apply the information you've learned in this book as soon as you're able. Every time you realign after being triggered; you've overcome the old self.

Knowledge, in of itself, doesn't teach anyone anything. The words in this book are merely doorways of opportunity; it is you who must walk through them by applying it. When you apply this knowledge, it becomes *wisdom*. You can only know these truths through experience; there's no point in memorising these teachings if you're not going to apply them; their application is essential.

"Let us not love in words or speech, but with actions and in truth."
– John 3:18

You're already everything you desire to be. This book isn't about becoming anything; it's designed to help you drop those ideas that contradict your true nature. In doing so, the light of your soul can shine unrestricted; get *ready* to embrace your innate perfection.

Also, this book may seem repetitive, but that's because I want to drill this information into your subconscious. You'll soon come to know the book inside out; and the more you know it, the easier you'll be able to put it into practice. Memorisation is an *essential* aspect of the doing process.

Finally, I wish to extend my appreciation to you for having the courage to not only face that which contradicts your truth but for also being brave enough to express it. In love and gratitude, I hope you find this book beneficial to your development.

THE MEDITATIVE LIFE

The mind is full of complexities, even more so when fear-based beliefs are hijacking your perception. This book will help you integrate your unconscious beliefs, *loosening* the mind's obsessive need to control every aspect of your life in the process.

The mind is an instrument we use to focus our consciousness in physical reality, but it has hijacked people's lives due to their fear of the unknown. When the stress response is activated, your mind scans your environment to avoid any potential dangers to the self. To live a meditative life, embracing the unknown is *essential* but it is impossible to do so when you're perceiving reality through a fear-based lens!

"In between each and every thought is a space, and that is where freedom lies, in experiencing this space. How simple it is to experience it! Anyone can do it, and yet, staying in that experience of space can be so hard. Are you able to experience that space and the sense of spaciousness that comes from that for a moment?"

– Gina Lake, Ten Teachings for One World

The more aware a person becomes, the more they become engrossed in the present moment throughout their day. Fear becomes less dominant in the life of a meditator as they enjoy the *simplicity* of their natural state.

Being present should be natural, effortless; one becomes absorbed in the present moment when they do what they love without expectations. It is essential to engage in activities that fan the flames of your joy, love, and bliss. In following your passion, by doing what you love, you embody the state where the illusions of the past have no power over you. The habitual performance of actions which generate bliss, peace, and love is *the key* to living in the here and now.

Even though your presence shouldn't be dependent solely on your actions; you should be able to enter the state while doing nothing, but this gets the ball rolling. Eventually, the presence you feel while writing or painting, for example, will start to seep into *everything* you do.

"O Arjuna! That man succeeds supremely who, by disciplining the senses, remains non-attached and keeps his organs of activity steadfast on the path of God-reminding activities."
– Bhagavad Gita 3:7

Living in the present also brings up the perceptions that aren't aligned with your true self. When you become *conscious* of these misaligned beliefs, you need to know how to integrate the emotions generated by them. The contrast these fear-based emotions give you is an important aspect of the process; to discover what you are, you must experience what you're not, first by contrast.

Before we can let go of anything, we must shine the light of our consciousness onto it. The impressions drilled in our mind by society is often the root cause of our anguish. Releasing them is fundamental to realising the true self.

In freeing yourself from the fear-based shackles, you'll be more capable of living in the present without the inner resistance that usually surfaces when you try to embody your natural state. Let the embodiment of this state become effortless by doing what you love without expectations. Acting on your passion anchors you into that flow-zone; the action itself becomes your reward.

It's impossible to have expectations when you're truly present. Freeing yourself from these false expectations liberates you from the constraints your mind has on your reality as the higher self can then manifest the outcomes you *need*. When you meditate, for example, it should be done, as Krishna teaches in the Gita, without expectation; have no ulterior motive other than to embody your true self.

Understanding the purpose of the physical mind is the key to experiencing the peace of God that *passeth all understanding*.

When you're calm, the intuitive wisdom of the higher self can guide you. The intent of this book is to relieve the mind of the extra responsibility you unconsciously give it by merging it with the intelligence of the higher self.

ABUNDANCE

Many in our society, equate abundance with money and possessions, but to me, true abundance is a peace and joy independent of outer circumstances.

How many billionaires are truly at peace within themselves? Howard Hughes, who was the richest man in the world at one point, admitted that his wealth failed to deliver him true happiness. He attained vast resources, but his mind still troubled him daily. Why? Most likely because, and others like him, realised that it's impossible to purchase true freedom; money can't buy you love.

"The disunited (one not established in the true self) doesn't have wisdom or meditation. To the unmeditative, there is no tranquillity. Without peace, how is true happiness possible?"
—*Bhagavad Gita 2: 66*

Inner peace must be your priority because, without it, you can't enjoy anything in life. I'd rather have a tranquil mind over anything the world can offer me. When you know how to embody your natural state; you also attract the outer forms of abundance you need.

Many chase fulfilment in things that go against their truth and this is because, on some level, they believe they require these experiences to feel complete. The incompleteness is an illusion; however, as everyone is already whole within themselves, they just believe the opposite.

Thoughts, feelings, and beliefs form the foundation of our persona, which generates our behaviour. The vibration we emit via our state of being is mirrored back at us in the outer world.

Ultimately, there is no external world; all you behold, out there, are the workings of your mind crystallised into form.

"Be not deceived; God is not mocked: for whatsoever a man soweth, that shall he also reap."
– Galatians 6:7

If you wish to attract money, for example, you must think, feel, believe, and behave like you already have it. You must lock into the state of being of the person you desire to be, but how does one feel like they have money before it manifests? The key is to understand that there is no before and after. Linear time is an illusion; all potential realities exist *now* in suspended animation, waiting for your choices to bring them unto life. If you're capable of imagining a specific reality, then that reality must exist on some level, as everything in physical reality is a figment of your imagination.

People's definition of abundance needs to be re-examined, however, because you can be financially wealthy and still be poor in spirit. You're also capable of feeling well-off without a penny to your name!

The purpose of this book is to highlight these outdated definitions which will enable you to see that your reality is a lot more malleable than you may believe. Once you discover your creative power through your connection to the source, you become the wealthiest person in the universe. Jesus likened the kingdom of God to the Pearl of Great Price; when you find this pearl, no circumstance can take it away from you.

"The game of life is a game of boomerangs. Our thoughts, deeds and words return to us sooner or later with astounding accuracy."
– Florence Scovel Shinn

We're already as powerful as we'll ever be and, on some level, we create every aspect of our lives. Sometimes, we create consciously, other times, unconsciously. All we experience is the result of what we're putting out into the universe via our state of being or the karma we've agreed to before birth; you can't be more abundant than that! It's empowering to realise your innate abundance by honing in your ability to create your life *consciously.*

People would achieve so much more in life if they understood that at each moment, they have the ability to do what they need to do. If you're always given what you need (not what you want), how can you be more abundant than that? When you feel lacking, remind yourself that this moment is sufficient unto itself.

Abundance comes in many forms; the key is to expand your definition of the concept in general. In whichever way you desire to be abundant, it's essential to feel as if you already are, because, in truth; you're everything you could ever want and more. Embody wholeness consistently, and you may be pleasantly surprised when wealth, health, and wisdom come looking for *you*. If you're having difficulty embodying your natural state, then it's time to explore your emotions to uncover the beliefs preventing you from doing so!

Please refer to the ***beliefs*** section for assistance in bringing your limiting beliefs into conscious awareness.

Fear reflects what you believe to be true the moment it arises. So, if you're feeling anxious, for example, it's time to start exploring your feelings to find out why. Unconscious beliefs don't reveal themselves on their own; you must discover them yourself through honest methods of introspection.

"You are not a drop in the ocean; you are the ocean within a drop."

– Rumi

One of the best ways to feel your innate abundance is to remind yourself of how your very existence is a blessing. Feel your body from within; look up at the night sky; gaze at the stillness and unrivalled beauty of the moon and the stars; inhale gratitude and exhale joy. Feel the wondrous mystery of creation and how our existence is a miracle in of itself.

Also, remember you don't need to base your sense of abundance on the things you possess. The real wealth is in your connection to the source as a wave on its infinite ocean. Through this connection, you discover your joy, worth, and all the other forms of abundance you need.

"But seek ye first the kingdom of God, and his righteousness and all these things shall be added unto you."

– Matthew: 6:33

Jesus nailed it in this verse; true abundance comes from the depths of your own heart. In essence, he's saying that your inner world is the primary reality and the outer world is a reflection of it. Go *within*, all the answers to your questions are there; waiting for you to find them. When one is in communion with the depths of their being; they let go and trust that life will bring them what they need in perfect timing. They hand over the reins to the higher self, which guides them to the fulfilment of their destiny.

"The superconscious mind is the God Mind within each man and is the realm of perfect ideas. In it, is the 'perfect pattern' spoken of by Plato, The Divine Design; for there is a Divine Design for each person."
– Florence Scovel Shinn

Yoga (union with the divine) occurs when you surrender to the perfect pattern in your consciousness. The divine design blossoms within you when you merge with the superconscious, which is the level of your being transcendent of linear space-time; thus, it would be *wise* for you to tap into it. Drop the need to know how things will unfold by embracing the unknown and allow the higher self to manifest the forms of abundance you need.

Affirmations

Everybody talks to themselves; if not vocally, they certainly do mentally. The conversations we have with ourselves play a significant role in the signs and circumstances that manifest in our life. Our self-talk reflects what we believe to be true about ourselves and the world around us. Belief systems are the building blocks of our reality; they determine the scope through which we filter our experiences.

Every time you speak, mentally or vocally; you're affirming; this is why the sages of Ancient India, for example, instructed their disciples to be mindful of their thoughts, actions and speech. If one misuses these powers, they attract situations to reflect the negativity they're putting out into the universe; all is a reflection.

"Your word is your wand."
– Florence Scovel Shinn

Words can be dangerous if they are uttered unconsciously; our word is everything. It's essential to guard against careless and lethargic talking; we must be mindful of what we're saying and the definitions we use to explain ideas and concepts when interacting with others. While speaking, it's important to be calm and to speak with care and respect.

Word is within the word, *sword* for a reason; if you speak to others in a degrading fashion, then your tongue, which is sharper than any sword, can inflict deep wounds in their psyche. Be mindful of how you interact with others because, in essence, they're an aspect of yourself. When you harm another, you're harming yourself; only hurt people hurt others.

"Talking to oneself is a habit everyone indulges in, we can no more stop talking to ourselves than we could stop eating and drinking. All we can do is control the nature and direction of our inner conversation."
– Neville Goddard

Misuse of *the word* is one of the reasons why our world is in the state we find it in today. Many purposely condition those around them through their harsh, cruel and belittling speech. When interacting with others, it's important to consider the soul of the person before you; empathy costs nothing but your ego.

Affirmations are powerful tools, as they can remind you of your true nature. When a person is depressed or anxious, a veil of forgetfulness *clouds* their perception; they forget everything they know while living in survival.

When using positive and dynamic affirmations, speak them with all your willpower; *feel* them into being. The subconscious must be impressed as you use them; if you're not feeling what you're affirming, then you don't believe the affirmation. Your conviction generates feelings; in this respect, feeling *is* believing. Emotions reflect what you believe to be true the moment they arise.

"You will be a failure until you impress the subconscious with the conviction you are a success. This is done by making an affirmation which clicks."
– Florence Scovel Shinn

If you desire to impress your subconscious with an affirmation but are having difficulty, then you probably have negative beliefs hijacking your perception counteracting it. It's crucial to bring these beliefs into awareness and recognise their falsehoods, which will enable you to impress the affirmation on your subconscious.

Using affirmations mentally can be a liberating tool but voicing them is powerful. Your self-talk is one of the building blocks of your subjective reality. If the idea of using affirmations excites you, I suggest you speak your favourite ones into existence daily. If done correctly, you'll behold the magic of your word as you watch your reality to bend to it.

Most have an abundance of negative thoughts playing on repeat in their head. It's important not to resist these thoughts; what do I mean? I'm saying you shouldn't react to them out of fear, as they are simply residue from what you *believe* is your past. They only determine your state of being if you allow them. Learn to laugh at the lies in your mind and remember how cherished and supported you are by the divine. To forgive is to forget the past and move forward. Nothing goes away until it's shown you what it needs to. It is only when the lies between your ears no longer trigger you have you realised freedom.

Most of the thoughts that spin on the carousel of your mind aren't *relevant* to who you are today. You're holding onto them because you believe that what they are saying is true, or in other words, you're allowing them to define you. When you resist anything in life; you reinforce it, as you're giving it more of your energy than it needs. Nonattachment to your thoughts is one of the benefits of meditation. Allow the illusory clouds of the past to come and go without fear and eventually, they'll lose their momentum as you're no longer resisting them. Negative thoughts are rendered powerless by your refusal to believe them.

In the meditative state, you carefully observe your thoughts, and over time become familiar with the patterns in your mind; this is why the Tibetan definition of the word meditation is to become *familiar with*.

Acknowledge the thoughts that scare you; don't deny them, because your resistance patterns are great teachers. They can be used as messengers, helping you discover the beliefs playing hide and seek in your unconscious. Observe your thoughts diligently, because once you realise why they are there, you'll have an easier time becoming indifferent to them.

> ***"Resistance is Hell, for it places man in a state of torment."***
> ***– Florence Scovel Shinn***

The more aware you become, the more you see all the choices you could potentially make in life; positive and negative. Learning how to not resist anything within you is a spiritual practice in of itself; it shows you that everything is a choice. You don't have to accept every offer your mind presents you with, to do so would be insanity, as it is full of contradictions. Non-resistance is the key to liberation from compulsive thinking.

We contain infinite possibilities within us, and if this is true, then those potentials must belong to both sides of the coin. Allow all choices to be and then choose the reality you prefer without resisting what you don't. When you cease resisting darkness, you'll behold the light more clearly, because resistance reinforces what you don't want and distorts your perception. Your shadow is the contrast that enables you to choose your truth; if used correctly, it serves you.

When negative thoughts disturb you, write them down on a piece of paper and ask yourself:

"Why are these thoughts in my mind? What beliefs are they showing me? What past experiences are they reflecting?"

Fear gets such a bad rap because it's uncomfortable, but it's a natural emotion; we have it for a reason. When you make it a valid aspect of the human condition, then you can use it for its intended purpose; to help you discover more of your true self. Your fear isn't a problem; the issue is your *fear* of fear. You're afraid of it because you believe it shouldn't be there, but if that were true, then it wouldn't be.

Affirm what you are; cease falling for the same old subconscious tricks that keep you on the merry-go-round of misery. Make it a habit to affirm your truth, and your life will blossom magically. Speak peace into existence for those who are dear to you; declare *divine* abundance, true wealth for everyone.

ANGER

Anger is a huge challenge to many, even those who rarely succumb to the emotion, have to associate with people who often do. We live in an angry society, with many projecting their frustrations onto one another. Hardly anyone has found inner peace, except those who do the work of integrating their shadow rather than suppressing it.

Anger is an emotion associated with pain and frustration, which stems from your attitude towards life; what you believe about yourself and how you're perceiving the situation when it arises.

There are two forms of anger, just and fear-based. Make no mistake about it, the ego in many is very cunning; they know exactly what they're doing; they'll attempt to walk all over you if you're not careful by taking advantage of your generosity. Being spiritual doesn't mean you become a doormat for others. Sometimes, it's necessary to defend yourself; otherwise, they'll continue trying to use you as a means to an end.

It's rare, but if the occasion calls for you to stick up for yourself or another you see being mistreated, then its fine to express how you feel. If physical violence breaks out, then breathe deeply and remove yourself from the situation. There are even times when it's necessary to defend yourself against someone who is physically attacking you, but you'll have a better chance of doing so if you're inwardly calm.

The yogic concept *Ahimsa* (non-violence) was something Mahatma Gandhi practised, even when he was shot by his murderer by telling him that he forgave him. He believed that if people were attacking us that we shouldn't defend ourselves. Paramahansa Yogananda, challenged his perspective on the concept, however, by asking him what he'd do if someone came into his village with a shotgun and started killing people. Gandhi's response was: "I'd lay down my own life."

This approach isn't the true meaning of non-violence. Ahimsa means to remove the *desire* to do harm to any living creature, but it doesn't mean you shouldn't kill harmful insects when necessary, for example. When one of those awful school shootings happens, the police officers have no choice but to kill the shooter, otherwise they'd kill more people! Simply giving your life away to someone who'd just as easily take more isn't a very smart or righteous thing to do.

Many murderers and abusers are born through anger, perpetrated rashly by those who did things which they, later, lived to regret. Christ was angry when he destroyed the marketplace in the temple. He and his disciples went in there and crashed the entire place! I'm sure a master like Jesus was in complete control of his emotions and knew what he was doing, however.

Peace is far *superior* to anger; approaching people through the soothing balm of love, understanding and peace is the best way to resolve any dispute. Never to allow the negative actions of others to determine your state of being.

Consciously *choose* peace. Even if you're to choose righteous anger, you must do so with awareness; never be thrown into it by another's unconsciousness, because the moment you are, you've become unconscious yourself.

The negative side of anger is the frustration that arises when your expectations or assumptions have fallen short. When you live in expectation of a much-anticipated future, but life doesn't turn out the way you hoped, frustration can arise. It's much better to live in the present moment with the understanding that life is *full* of surprises. Things hardly ever turn out the way you expect them to. Realise this and breathe it in deeply; God's ways are not our own.

Many react on autopilot when things don't go their way. The trigger could be small or life-threatening, but they respond in the same old way. Your quality of life improves when you take responsibility for your state of being. Until you accept that not everything will go the way you want it to in life, then the frustration will continue to arise in you. You came to this world to master your energy and every challenge you overcome awakens more of your innate divinity. In passing such tests, you'll be on the path to mastery of your inner and outer worlds, which you will realise are identical.

Do you believe things should always go your way? Do you think you shouldn't consider others when your emotions get the better of you? Do you think you can't control yourself? There are many definitions attached to anger that convince people they're not in control, but the only person in control of your life is *you*. If you're generating fear, then you must be creating it. The environment doesn't create emotions; it's your *perception* of it that does.

Even your most outrageous display of anger was, on some level, a *choice*. You unconsciously defined the circumstance in a way that it provoked you. It's essential to bring these beliefs and definitions into awareness to avoid such scenarios because until you do, they'll continue to control your behaviour.

"You will not be punished for your anger, you will be punished by your anger."
– Buddha

Fear-based emotions aren't supposed to enslave you; you're to be their master. They exist to show you that you're buying into ideas that don't belong to you. At whatever rate you're comfortable, feel into them and breathe deeply; take a step back, see the forest from the trees; realise that they are a choice, on some level, even if it's an unconscious one. The first time you see that your anger is a choice may surprise you, but if you keep practising, it will become easier to handle.

Change your attitude towards life; cease attempting to control every aspect of it out of fear; it doesn't work anyway; your attempts are in *vain*. Learn to let go when you need to, and drop your assumptions related to how you believe your life *should* unfold. Learn how to flow with the river, because, paradoxically, you can only surrender to the control within you by letting go. The river only flows one way; you can either flow with it or against it; the choice is yours.

ANXIETY

Many struggle with anxiety nowadays. They must learn how to manage their emotions because ignoring them only makes things worse in the long run. There's nothing wrong with being triggered into anxiety; it's an emotion we all feel from time to time; it is a form of fear, and fear can be a great teacher if you're willing to *accept* it.

It's common nowadays to be prescribed medication by your doctor to numb yourself from your fear. Even though this method may serve some, I believe it should be a temporary option at best. Years ago, when I suffered from a relentless form of hypochondria, I was prescribed diazepam by my doctor; they made me feel worse!

Some conditions do require psychotropic drugs to keep a person stable, but people, in general, aren't meant to be dependent on pills for the rest of their lives. Medication should be combined with therapy, counselling, meditation or mindfulness to help the person understand what's going on inside them. When they know the *root* of their anxiety instead of just believing they're stuck, they can start rebuilding their inner world with positivity and loving support from their family and friends; I write from experience.

The hypothalamus in the brain secretes hormones, known as *neuropeptides*, for every emotional state experienced in the body. There are peptides to match anger, anxiety, frustration; there are also peptides that match elevated emotions such as joy, love, and appreciation. Our beliefs trigger emotions in the body, and after buying into lies that arouse the stress response for years, we become chemically addicted to them.

So many are chronically anxious as they're addicted to stress hormones. Anything we do repeatedly becomes subconscious and automatic; this is what has happened with those suffering from chronic forms of stress and anxiety. They're buying into a bundle of beliefs that convince them to be defined by the past, fear the unknown, and have zero faith in their process.

The focus of this book is identifying these beliefs, bringing them into awareness, releasing them and then anchoring yourself in your natural, heart-centred state of being. If you keep overcoming your conditioning and returning home to your true self; it will eventually become second nature.

Anxiety is a form of resistance; observe it diligently. Your triggers are messengers, pointing you to the beliefs hijacking your perception. When you start the work of integrating these emotions, they may amplify at first; but will dissolve when they've shown you what they need to.

Many use illegal substances or alcohol to numb themselves from their fear-based emotions. We've just entered a new decade, and the energies are intensifying to bring out people's inner demons like never before; it's time, my friends, to take *responsibility* for your state of being. Pull the sword of your creative power out of the inertia of society's beliefs and align your perception with the reality you prefer.

When you first notice that the outer world mirrors your state of being, you'll realise that it *always* has. At this point, there will be nowhere to run, nowhere to hide, but at least you can begin creating consciously, fasten your seatbelt and enjoy the ride. Everyone has this experience at some point. When you realise that you've always been creating your reality, but have done so unconsciously, it can be hard to accept. Don't beat yourself up, though; at least you know the truth now, which is all that matters.

"Yesterday I was clever, so I wanted to change the world. Today I am wise, so I am changing myself."
– Rumi

If you fear the unknown, then it's important to question your beliefs about it because until you do, you'll always resist the unfamiliar. The unknown is the only place you'll find your true self. In the known, you've discovered parts of yourself; the rest of you is in uncharted territory, waiting for you to find it. You've already looked in your comfort zone; it's time to embrace the unfamiliar to discover the rest of you. Nothing halts progress more than staying in the prickled nest of the familiar to feel safe; the truth is you *never* grow when you're comfortable.

The biggest addiction isn't drugs or alcohol but fear itself. Many claim to fear darkness, but this isn't true; as they're comfortable wallowing in their false self. People indulge in fear-based emotions so much that they become their biggest addiction and the root of their other crutches.

People don't fear darkness, they fear the light, the unknown, as they know their true self is there, but won't go looking for it because they're afraid to face themselves. Most wear masks to conform to the beliefs of those around them, but by doing so, they never realise their potential.

It's time to rip these masks off your face; they don't belong to you, they never did. Cease trying to be someone you're not; there's nothing more exhausting than this; it's why you feel *weighed down*. When you're aligned with your soul, you feel as light as a feather; you're calm, at peace and trust where life is taking you.

Befriend your anxiety. Every person on this planet feels fear from time to time; it's all good. Become aware of the patterns and the beliefs reinforcing them. The key to wisdom is to *know* yourself; when a man knows himself, he comes to know the world.

APPRECIATION

An attitude of gratitude is fundamental on the spiritual path; not only does it enable you to perceive the beauty in all before you; but it also brings you more reasons to be thankful. The outer world responds to our state of being; if this principle is true, then consistently feeling gratitude must bring *more* blessings into our life.

When you're feeling low, one of the best things you can do to investigate why is to *raise* your vibration. Reminding yourself of all the good things in your life is the best place to start. When you fall in vibration, a veil of forgetfulness clouds your perception. Lower-vibratory states can be shaken off by merely remembering how blessed you are.

It may take a while to train yourself to be grateful for everything in life but remember that repetition rewires the subconscious. If you feel gratitude, a few times a day, every day, the state will eventually become second nature. Appreciation boosts the immune system and resets the baseline in the amygdala; living in gratitude from your heart centre is the key to health, wellbeing and longevity.

According to neuroscience, the average person lives in the stress response during 70% of their day. Appreciation not only helps you relax but also enables you to see how your anxiety is an illusion. The higher you're vibrating, the more you're able to observe what's going on inside you. The answers you seek are always *up* the vibrational scale; never down. Accepting your fear-based emotions is pivotal to this process; their acceptance raises your vibration.

If you're struggling to feel appreciation at this moment, you're either taking things for granted or allowing the lies between your ears to define you. Maybe it's the way you're labelling the circumstance at hand? Realise this; when you change the way you look at things, what you're looking at changes; the moment you change your state of being, you see things differently.

Also, appreciating the people in your life is essential to embodying an attitude of gratitude. Cherish them, as you never know when it's the last time, you'll see them; life is so unpredictable. Show them with your actions, how much you appreciate their presence, and especially your lover if you're in an intimate relationship.

"If the only prayer you said in your whole life was, 'thank you,' that would suffice."
– Meister Eckhart

There are many techniques you can use to remind yourself to be more grateful in your day-to-day life. Use your imagination to conjure up ways you can do this. Maybe you can place signs that say appreciation or gratitude around your home or workspace or keep an object in your pocket that reminds you to say thank you every time you touch it; it's up to you. The American tradition of saying grace before dinner is a reminder to embody appreciation, but you can also say thank you before doing other things as well; assign the practice to *everything* you do.

I recommend living in an attitude of gratitude as much as possible. Get in touch with how miraculous life is; how lucky we are to be alive. Remind yourself how much more fortunate you are than those struggling with poverty, starvation and famine in third world countries. Not appreciating what you have while entire nations are malnourished is selfish. The average person has so much before them they don't see because they take things for granted. When you start appreciating the simple things, you'll live a happy and joy-filled life. If you don't acknowledge what you already have, why would the universe give you more?

ASSUMPTIONS

Fear-based assumptions are detrimental to one's health and spiritual growth. All circumstances are neutral until defined by the mind, which often automatically assigns limiting definitions onto everything. People perceive reality through the scope of a persona shaped by past experiences, which distorts their perception of the present. Assumptions reflect the beliefs in the unconscious; when you live in survival, the mind relentlessly scans your environment for potential threats.

Until the mind merges with the higher self by surrendering its need to control every aspect of your life; it will resist the unknown. The conditioned persona has many ways of convincing you to avoid the unknown; it uses fear-based assumptions to protect itself.

When one buys into beliefs that devalue their worth, they fear anything new entering their lives. They'll avoid things they usually wouldn't avoid and assume most circumstances pose a threat to their survival. Because they persisted in these assumptions, they wind up creating experiences they were trying to avoid. Assumptions are beliefs; what you assume is happening *reflects* where your conviction lies.

"An assumption, though false, if persisted in, will harden into fact."
– Neville Goddard

The good news is that you can use these assumptions to your advantage. Circumstances usually only trigger you if you unconsciously *assume,* they pose a threat to your wellbeing. When you're triggered, sit, breathe and accept the emotion; allow it to be with the knowledge that it has something valuable to teach you. As you go into the feeling, enter a curious state and ask yourself questions along the lines of:

"What must I believe to generate this assumption? Why do I believe the worst is going to happen? What am I assuming at this moment?"

These questions will help you identify your resistance, as fear-based assumptions are resistance to what is. Once you've integrated the emotion, open your eyes and embrace the present moment. Tranquillity begets *clarity*; when you're calm, the higher self infuses your thoughts with its intelligence; you see things for what they are.

As I said in the introduction; repetition *rewires* the subconscious mind. When you master the art of redefining circumstances from a tranquil state, you'll realise how the outer world bends to your perception.

The awakening process is a continuous oscillation from the inertia of the old self to the true self, which is *fluid* like water; morphing itself to embrace any situation life pours it in. The length of this process is as long as it needs to be, so learn to enjoy it. Every aspect of your shadow dissolves once it's taught you what it needs to. The process of peeling away these layers is why we came here; allow it to be.

In becoming aware of the impact your definitions have on your reality, you create with precision. You cease allowing the environment to determine your state of being, which is the opposite of a victim mentality. On the level of the ego, you may not always be in control of what happens, but you're certainly in control of *how* you respond to it.

Assumptions are unconscious defence mechanisms to protect the ego from the unknown; it likes to be in control of every aspect of your life. When given too much responsibility, though, it tires under pressure because it's incapable of doing the job of the higher self. The true role of the ego is to perceive what's happening in the present moment; thus, you'll only be capable of using it properly when you *trust* in life.

The higher self is the real you; it can see the big picture and knows why things happen the way they do. Not one fear-based assumption is from the higher self; they are simply the mind's way of distorting the present so it can hold onto what's familiar because it fears the unknown.

There's also a creative way to use the power of assumption, as our assumptions are beliefs, and beliefs are the building blocks of our subjective reality. When you desire something; assume you already have it to bring it into manifestation, because as Goddard says; assumptions harden into fact if persisted.

Let's say you want to go to Tokyo, Japan. You have no money but have a deep yearning to go there. All you need to do is assume you're already there. I don't mean thinking about being there but go *beyond* what your senses are telling you. You want to be in Japan, but your senses are elsewhere. What would you be feeling if you were walking around Tokyo? Close your eyes and *feel* your excitement as you explore areas such as Shinjuku, Akihabara, and Shibuya. When you go to bed, fall asleep in the assumption that you're sleeping in Tokyo. The key is to do this every night until your dream becomes a reality. Don't think of how it will come to pass but have the mindset that it has already. If you can imagine being in Tokyo, then you're already there. Embodying the state aligned with that reality shifts you to it.

"The first thing you do, you must know exactly what you want in this world. When you know exactly what you want, make as life-like a representation as possible of what you would see, and what you would touch, and what you would do were you physically present and physically moving in such a state."
– Neville Goddard

Your imagination is your creative power; everything you can imagine exists in some reality. You're already who you desire to be and connecting to the state of being of that version of you pulls you toward them.

"You know, there is a wide difference between thinking OF what you want in this world and thinking FROM what you want."
– Neville Goddard

Desires come to fruition if you believe they will. Assumptions can be used to manifest anything you desire.

Unfortunately, most are assuming in an unconscious, fear-based way; taking themselves to realities, they don't prefer. Assume you're healthy, abundant and, as Rumi said; that the universe is *rigged* in your favour and it shall be.

AWAKENING

Many assume they're awakening because they've read a bunch of articles on social media. This may give one a more holistic approach to what's happening in society, but has *no* relation to spiritual awakening, which occurs within oneself.

One starts to awaken when they're ready. After years of false promises from the world, their focus reverts *inwards* to discover their wholeness, which never left them. They just believed they were incomplete because they bought into the lies between their ears. They also have the realisation that they are solely responsible for their happiness; they cease using people as a means to an end.

"Let nothing disturb you, let nothing frighten you. All things are passing away: God never changes. Patience obtains all things. Whoever has God lacks nothing; God alone suffices."
– St Teresa of Avila

The awakening process is no joke, but also the biggest laugh! To awaken takes the courage to unearth the lies that have hijacked your perception, perhaps for decades. It requires the bravery to admit who you've been up to this moment in your life. The awakening soul is open to learning and expanding their consciousness; they've become conscious of their connection with their higher self. As a result, they're receptive to any subliminal messages the universe sends them through the synchronicity that appears in their lives.

A state of heightened receptivity is the foundation of the awakened soul's life. They're open to learning and admitting they're wrong when they are. They also know that they know nothing, and that consciousness never stops expanding. They trust the way their life unfolds and deal with their resistance patterns as they emerge.

"The key is to move inward where you can explore your inner world. Your Inner world is so vast beyond your imagination. You are carrying the whole universe within you, but you are not aware of this. Even your God resides within you. Move inward, explore that inner world."

– Guru Ma, Ritu

Many use spirituality as a fad, to appear superior in the eyes of onlookers. Oblivious to the true purpose of the spiritual path, they fail to reach the depths of their soul. When their shadow, in the form of fear-based perceptions and intense emotions come to the surface to be dealt with, they resort to substances such as drugs or alcohol to suppress it. The awakening process is the gradual release of everything we've unconsciously defined as ourselves; this requires, not only immense courage but faith that borders on *unshakable*!

Some awaken after a profoundly life-shattering experience, such as an out-of-body experience or in some cases, a near-death experience. For most, their process is gradual; their pain comes up in waves to be accepted. As time goes by, they progressively become more integrated, awakened to their true self.

BELIEFS

Belief systems are the building blocks of our physical reality experience. The way we perceive reality reflects our state of being. We filter the environment through the scope of our beliefs and definitions which overlap our windows of perception.

Many are realising the profound influence of their beliefs and the impact they have on their lives. We perceive reality in conjunction with our emotional state; we see things as we are, as all things in creation are neutral until perceived by an observer. The word *karma* has many negative connotations associated with it, but it's merely this law; the outer world bends to your perception of it.

For most, many of their beliefs are unconscious, which means they're not aware that they are buying into them. There are two kinds of belief systems: positive (expansive) and negative (limiting). Positive beliefs reinforce our faith; they empower us to embrace the unknown without fear and initially fuel the desire to connect to the source within ourselves. Negative beliefs, on the other hand, inflict limitations on our creative power; they are the source of a confined mindset and are the origin of most of our struggles in life. All our fears and doubts, when investigated with awareness, lead us to the unconscious acceptance of a limiting belief.

The planets, Jupiter, and Saturn, represent this duality in the science of Astrology. Jupiter is the great benefic; he represents the expansion of consciousness; faith and the source itself. Saturn represents one's time-bound conditioning, limitations and the contrast required to perceive the truth. In Greek mythology, Saturn is Jupiter's father; he ate many of his children and thought he'd also eaten Jupiter, but his wife tricked him. After being saved by his mother, Jupiter grew up and overthrew his wicked father. The meaning behind this story is that consciousness (the source) always overcomes linear space-time illusions (Chronos, Saturn). All experiences in the physical realm are transitory; they don't touch the pure consciousness of the soul; which is ever-existing, ever-consciousness, ever-new bliss.

"Believe nothing, no matter where you read it or who has said it, not even if I have said it, unless it agrees with your own reason and your own common sense."
– Buddha

The reason I wrote this book was to help people identify their limiting beliefs and realign their perception with the integrity of their soul. One who sincerely practices these teachings will become conscious of the fact that they've always been creating their life, but unconsciously for the most part. Peeling away these limiting beliefs from your perception will enable you to perceive the present moment without distortion; allowing the higher self to take the reins of the chariot of your being.

The expansion of consciousness is the amplification of your perspective as an individualised soul. When you expand your awareness beyond the five senses, you're able to perceive yourself within others; even those who aren't physically present. A master who realised Christ consciousness such as *Paramahansa Yogananda*, for example, often said that he felt the entire universe as his own body. He became one with all that is, was and ever will be on a conscious level; one with the body of Christ.

An important thing to understand about belief systems is that they do everything they can to keep you believing in them. What does this mean? It means that beliefs always make it seem as if they are only logical, obvious or possible choice by continuously trying to reinforce themselves in your mind. These reinforcement mechanisms, however, serve us, because, without them, we wouldn't be capable of creating our reality, as our perception would be too *malleable*; thus, our creation would be all over the place.

When you become conscious of a limiting idea you've been buying into for years; expect your body to resist the changes you're attempting to make. Quite often, the belief will trigger the stress response to reinforce itself further; the old self can only survive in the known, in your comfort zone; which is a fear-based state of being generated by a distorted perception. So, as you're in the process of changing a limiting perspective, it would also be wise to *expect* the synchronicities that manifest during the process to reflect the belief you want to change. Expect the lies to amplify; to do all they can to get you to justify, rationalise reasons why you should continue to perceive in the same old way.

The universe loves to make sure you're ready to expand beyond the scope of your present limitations. Once you've established a new, more uplifting belief, or decide to throw it out of the window altogether, you'll manifest a situation reflective of the old idea to test whether you've truly changed. How you respond is vital; when you stand unshaken amidst a circumstance that would usually reinforce the old belief; you've dissolved it.

Every time you respond differently to a circumstance or synchronicity attempting to reinforce an old belief; you're dissolving the old self. Repetition rewires the subconscious; the more you react correctly to these illusions, the quicker you'll dissolve your unconscious associations with them. Also, please remember to stay light-hearted throughout this process; it's simply a game you're playing with yourself. When you reach the point where you can laugh at the synchronicities trying to reinforce your old self, you're on your way to *blessedness*.

All beliefs can be changed, as it's you who created them in the first place; even if they came from the minds of others, because in essence; thy neighbour *is* thyself. Knowing that beliefs can be changed is key because believing they can't is a limitation and therefore, by definition, a negative belief system.

THE RULES OF THE GAME

The game of life has rules we've agreed to abide by before we were born. In the board game known as *snakes and ladders*; when your piece lands at the top end of a ladder, then it must slide to the bottom, this is a rule in this game. There are many rules to the game of life. For example, our bodies age and die; they also require oxygen, water and food to survive. Gravity keeps us rooted to the ground, enabling us to roam the earth without flying off into space. These laws override the impact our beliefs have on our reality. You may believe you can fly, but if you were to hurl yourself off a cliff; you'll probably (most certainly) die.

For centuries, people believed the earth was flat, but their belief didn't make it so. The astronomer Galileo became one of many so-called heretics who was sentenced to death during the Inquisition for suggesting that the earth orbits the sun and not the other way around!

Some have had life-changing encounters with UFOs and extraterrestrials, even though they never believed in such phenomena before their experiences. E.T contact happens for these people because it's in their karmic blueprint, regardless of their beliefs. Atheists have also had similar experiences, waking up from sleep earlier than usual to see an apparition of Christ or Mother Mary at the end of their bed. Predestined events such as these, usually have a radically transformative effect on the lives of those who have them. They manifest to realign them with their purpose.

Paradoxically, however, one's karma can also override the rules of the game! The lives of many saints and spiritual masters are full of incidents and stories that defy logic; most noticeably *Mahavatar Babaji*, the master of *Lahiri Mahasaya,* another great master in of himself. According to reports and eyewitnesses, Babaji has an eternal physical body that he can dissolve at will, and re-manifest whenever he desires. Beings of this nature are known as avatars, the descent of divinity into flesh or in other words, full incarnations of the divine.

Avatars are beyond the rules of the game; some are great world teachers whose example impacts billions after their mission on earth has concluded. Examples of avatars throughout history are *Jesus Christ, The Blessed Virgin Mary, Krishna, Rama, Buddha, Lao Tzu, Sri Anandamayi Ma* and *Paramahansa Yogananda,* with the latter two coming more recently.

"The northern Himalayan crags near Badrinarayan are still blessed by the living presence of Babaji, guru of Lahiri Mahasaya. The secluded master has retained his physical form for centuries, perhaps for millenniums. The deathless Babaji is an avatara. This Sanskrit word means 'descent'; its roots are ava, 'down', and tri, 'to pass'. In the Hindu scriptures, avatara signifies the descent of Divinity into flesh."

– *Paramahansa Yogananda, (Autobiography of a Yogi)*

St Teresa of Avila, the Catholic saint who lived in the 1500s, was often seen defying the laws of physics, especially gravity. She'd levitate, even when she didn't want to! Her body would hover in the air while she and her sisters were attending mass; she found it extremely embarrassing and had no idea why it was happening. The point I'm making is that it depends on the karma you've chosen on a soul level. What your true self wants, it will get one way or the other; *resistance is futile.*

MAKING THE UNCONSCIOUS, CONSCIOUS

For lasting change to occur, you must light a match in a dark place. Enlightenment is precisely this, enlightening the darkness of your unconscious with the light of your consciousness. How does one accomplish this?

Vibrationally speaking, the unconscious is the highest level in your physical mind. It is no coincidence that the calmer one is, the more one sees within themselves; clarity is a by-product of tranquillity. The unconscious is the storehouse of your belief systems.

Negative emotions, in any form, are the key to discovering the door to the unconscious. All fear-based emotions are what it says they are, fear. Accepting your feelings is the first step to integrating the beliefs that pertain to them. The fight or flight response is only triggered when you *think* you're in some form of danger; whether consciously or unconsciously. Human beings can switch on the stress response by believing the negativity between their ears even when there is no external threat.

When an unpleasant emotion arises in the body, take a couple of deep breaths and simply be with the feeling. *Accept* it in its totality; allow it to be there, as it is what the present moment contains; resistance will only make things worse. Anything you accept in life transforms, that is the beautiful thing about acceptance. After some time of breathing with the emotion, you should start to calm down. As you feel yourself relaxing and your vibration raising, with self-compassion and curiosity, ask yourself questions along these lines:

"What just triggered me? What do I believe is true? What belief is hijacking my perception? How am I misaligned? What must I believe is true to feel this way?"

Come up with questions more suitable if you don't resonate with any of the above. Asking yourself these questions will reveal the beliefs that triggered you. Don't be afraid of the answers when they come. Remember that all perspectives can be changed, regardless of how hideous they are. The moment you bring these misaligned perceptions into consciousness, you'll probably laugh at how nonsensical they are, and when you do, you can't possibly continue to buy into them. You dissolve these beliefs by *realising* their illogicality.

I tell you to accept the feeling and raise your vibration first because investigating your thoughts and emotions from a low vibration strengthens the incoherence in the brain. You're incapable of thinking beyond an emotional state until you bring consciousness into it, thus attempting to do so will only reinforce the negativity. Raising your vibration takes you out of the high-beta brain waves into mid-beta, which then, from a curious state, you'll be able to *identify* the scope through which you're filtering the outer world. High-beta brain waves keep you thinking, feeling and believing that you need to survive when there is often no threat. Knowing how to change your brain waves is *crucial*.

Sure, when we were cavemen and saw a T-Rex running at us, the stress response used up all our energy to help us survive; but as I mentioned before, we can switch it on merely by thinking about our fears. The average person spends around 70% of their day in high-beta brain wave patterns, and we wonder why the world is in the state it is today! People are motivated to survive and not *thrive* in their natural state.

Identifying these limiting beliefs is a liberating experience, as each one you prune from the garden of your mind makes space for the flowers of your integrity to blossom. Enjoy the process; see it as a game, as without challenges, life would be dull, would it not? Nothing frees you more than bringing your unconscious into consciousness. To do this, you must work *with* the contrast in you; this simple technique helps you do just that.

CORE BELIEFS

Core beliefs produce many subsequent beliefs. As you identify limiting beliefs, you'll see that many of them have something in common; this will help you find the core belief spawning them. In modern cognitive behaviour therapy (CBT), they are known *schemas*. When you dissolve a core belief, the ideas associated with it dissolve along with it.

In some cases, a rebirth occurs when one transforms a core belief. They feel like a new person; their personality becomes so refined that they don't recognise who they used to be. Some prefer to chop away the branches of the tree before attempting to cut down the trunk, and others prefer the opposite way of transforming their core belief; whatever way works for you is the best way to go about it. In the book of Revelation, there is an allegory for core beliefs in chapter 13:

"The dragon stood on the shore of the sea. And I saw a beast coming out of the sea. It had ten horns and seven heads, with ten crowns on its horns, and on each head a blasphemous name."

– Revelation 13:1

The beast on the shore of the sea (emotions) is the core belief; its seven heads, and ten crowns on its horns, symbolise subsequent negative beliefs. The blasphemous names represent lies, illusions, and falsehoods. They are the beliefs that convince us that we're separate from the divine and that we're unworthy of love.

Nothing is outside of you; see the beliefs for the lies that they are and laugh when you succumb to the temptation of believing them. There are many perspectives to choose from; you don't have to accept the ones that limit and degrade you. Realign with your truth when you notice yourself buying into them. Also, it's fine to oscillate from the old self to your true self; trust in the process, and you'll master the art *knowing* when you're in tune and when you're not.

When you discover some of your limiting beliefs, it would be wise to write them down. Below them, perhaps in a different-coloured pen, write the perspective you prefer instead (it's usually the opposite of the belief). This method is a useful way of pruning the lies out the garden of your mind. In a sense, it will act as a torch that enlightens the dark tomb of your unconscious every time you shine your attention on it. Once you've become aware of a limiting belief and realise that it is complete and utter falsehood; you've dissolved it. Realign with your truth; rekindle the fires of your faith and embrace the unknown; the portal to your true self.

You don't change by fighting the old self. Identifying its fear-based perceptions is necessary, but after doing that, you must put *all* your energy into embodying your ever-new self, which burns away the past in you.

When you live in the present moment, your inner self infuses your thoughts with its wisdom. All things exist in the window of the now, including all past and future versions of yourself. Close your eyes and imagine yourself ten years older, and that you've achieved all the things you want to in the coming decade. How would you feel? What would be in your heart? What would drive you to go even further? Emotionally align with that version; attune to their state of being, and you'll begin to live as if your dreams are *already* a reality.

So, if you've discovered a limiting belief system but are still feeling the same way, it's because other beliefs are reinforcing it that you've yet to bring into consciousness. You must be fully present as you observe the workings of your inner world, as you can't fix yourself with a mind plagued by illusions. Only in the light of your consciousness can you transcend everything you believed you were.

You'll always have a personality as a physical being, so design your perception with thoughts, feelings and beliefs that inspire and uplift everyone around you. Learn to activate your heart centre and live with love beaming out your core, so its rays enlighten the darkness in those close to you. When you live from your centre, with a coherent heart and brain working in tandem, you go *beyond* belief into the knowing that's always been inside you. Your truth is unshakable; if someone can take it away, then it isn't yours.

Christ taught his disciples to live by *faith*, which isn't the blind form of belief that religious people practice; it is the deep understanding that life is always supporting us in our endeavours. The way our lives are orchestrated; the cookie crumbs that appear from time to time as synchronicities to guide us—there is a knowing within us that transcends words; this is true faith.

Collectively speaking, we're ready to explore the mysteries of the universe. Humanity is on the verge of an explosion of Christ consciousness, which will connect everyone on a conscious level. People who speak online from different sides of the planet, for example, often feel each other's emotions. We are in the beginning stages, but our world is becoming *conscious*; more and more people are waking up; the party is happening on Mother Earth, it is *why* we incarnated at this time.

CHALLENGES

We undergo many kinds of challenges in our lifetime, and especially in our interactions with others, from intimate relationships, friendships, sibling rivalries, and so on. On an individual level, the process of integrating the trauma stored in our emotional body is the biggest challenge we face. This process varies from person to person as each of us has a different past and were born in various cultures; our upbringing is a direct reflection of our karma.

Challenges are necessary experiences all must go through in physical reality, as without them, there would be no growth or realisations. Nor would we have any desire to ascend to higher levels of consciousness. How would we refine our egos and obtain the awareness of our soul if nothing pushed or tested us in life?

The way we define life's challenges determines how we respond to them when they inevitably manifest in our lives. One could argue they are the sole reason we incarnated here because, in the higher realms, the degree of illusions necessary to have these kinds of challenges simply doesn't exist. Transforming the darkness that's eclipsed the light of our soul is the point of a physical incarnation. We're playing the game of the *alchemist*, transforming our consciousness in the process.

Being also an Astrologer and having observed many birth charts over the years, it's become obvious to me that we incarnate when the planets are in mathematical harmony with our karma. The birth chart is a blueprint of the themes we agreed to participate in during this life. So, it would be wise for you to accept things as they happen because resistance only makes situations *more* challenging!

"If you accept a problem rather than fighting or struggling with it, then you've solved half the problem."

– Guru Ma, Ritu

Many lose their cool when things don't go their way, crumbling whenever circumstances get even remotely challenging. Only a handful of people have trained themselves to stay calm and present amidst the fires of unpleasant situations. They're automatically thrust into anxiety, anger, panic, shunning the responsibility for their state of being in the process. When people live in survival, they revert into their automatic, subconscious processes. They must learn how to respond to the challenges at hand by facing them directly with awareness and vigour. We're only capable of making the right decisions when the mind is calm; tranquillity begets *clarity*.

All challenges are for our betterment; even if we don't see how the moment they arise. How many times have you looked back at some of the awful things that have happened to you and realised that without them, you wouldn't be where you are today? There is a bigger picture to all situations; you may not be able to stop the waves, but you *can* learn how to surf. Having this kind of awareness is one of the benefits to merging with the higher self.

When conflict arises between lovers; for example, on some occasions, one of the persons involved may feel inclined to jump ship. It's the norm for people in our society to unconsciously replicate each other, and more often than not, they follow the examples of those that don't serve their best interests. In my experience, an intimate relationship with the right person is going to bring up your baggage to be dealt with so you can move forward with your life. Our most intimate of partners and friends act as *mirrors*; they reflect the workings of our unconscious to us. One of the primary purposes of close relationships is the challenges that come along with them.

Many in our society don't want to face their challenges. It's common nowadays for people, after their relationship has dissolved, to quickly find another in an unconscious attempt to suppress the pain that resurfaced in the previous one. This avoidance may work for a while, but in this transitory realm, everything becomes *familiar* thus, changes. When the honeymoon period of the new relationship wears off, the skeletons hidden in their closet come back to haunt them, but with even more momentum.

"Let go or be dragged."
– Zen proverb

There is *no escaping* your challenges. You'll have to deal with them in one way or another. You may even forget all about them but, eventually, they come back and usually when you're least expecting it. Face them with excitement! Train your mind to see the challenges as exciting opportunities to reinforce the notion that you're not a victim, but *a victor!* The game of life would be boring without any challenges. So, obliterate any that dare crosses your path! You're more powerful than any obstacles that obstruct your way into the Promised Land, why? Because it's you who manifests them! Pull the sword of your creative power out the stone society's beliefs and create the life you desire.

Choice

Many in our society, especially those who struggle with anger, depression, jealousy and so on, don't believe they have a choice in the matter. They think their patterns are hereditary and that they're doomed to remain enslaved by them for the rest of their lives.

It's common nowadays for people who struggle to control their volatile emotions to be prescribed some form of medication to numb themselves from the ups and downs of life. Medication may help you feel better, but it doesn't heal the *core* of your issues. As I said in the anxiety chapter, I'm not discrediting this form of medicine, since it does help some. I do believe, however, that it should only be a temporary option for most, used to manage symptoms as they undergo therapy to investigate the unconscious processes at the root of their issues.

Science is revealing, through *epigenetics*, that changing your perception of life, literally rewrites the chemistry in your brain and body. When you elevate your state of being, you up-regulate your gene expression because you're signalling your genes to create proteins equal to your joy. Genes are protein producing machines, and proteins are responsible for the structure and function of your physical body. Your genes make proteins equal to your state of being, so when you live in survival, the proteins generated aren't of good quality, because the body has to use up all of its energy when it believes it needs to survive.

When you master the art of overcoming the old self by slowing down your brain waves and staying present, then the proteins created will begin to rebuild and restore your body. If you're genuinely passionate about making inner peace your priority; get ready, miraculous healings are on the way. Fear destroys, joy heals; it's *that* simple.

Cease believing you're stuck, because it's only your belief in this false notion that makes it seem so. You, as the physical self, get to *choose* how you respond to situations as they arise. Living without awareness is a sure-fire way of creating the experiences you don't prefer, as you unknowingly match the frequency of the things you're trying to avoid. Non-resistance is vital because fear is a state of being that is just as magnetic as peace and joy. The inner self can see the outcome of all the potential choices you could make; this is why some people get a hunch to do something that makes no sense, but it works out in the end. You can either embody *Hades*, the God of the underworld (unconsciousness) or *Minerva*, the Goddess of wisdom; every moment, the choice is yours.

People always feel motivated to do what they think serves them best. Those who have anger issues must believe, on some level, that projecting their problems onto others serves them in some way, shape or form. This kind of experience *can* be a positive one if they're willing to use it to become conscious of the beliefs generating the anger; otherwise, they'll continue making the same mistakes.

Maybe their anger is an unconscious defence mechanism to keep others at arm's length? Or they may be projecting their insecurities onto others because they're in denial of them? Until they enlighten the darkness of their inner world with the light of their consciousness, they'll never know why anger is predominant in them. The choice is *always* there to introspect, but most are either too lazy or lethargic to even try.

The beliefs we've harvested from the minds of others are also, on some level, a choice. Have we not chosen to buy into them? On a higher level of consciousness, we chose the city we'd be born into and even our parents. Everything we're experiencing is ultimately of our own doing. We weren't cast down here by some wrathful God. All the limitations we experience are self-imposed illusions. We chose to be here at this moment; our individualised consciousness is projecting it all.

Habits are another example of illustrating the fact that we're choosing more than we may believe. When someone realises that they have an addiction and continue to perpetuate it daily, they usually shrug their shoulders and say: "I can't help it! I don't have any control over myself!" If they're aware of the habit, however, then they must be *choosing* to prolong its stranglehold on their consciousness. They need to ask themselves *why* they believe perpetuating this pattern is a better alternative than change; just what are you getting out of it?

People must take *responsibility* for their choices. When a person recognises addictive patterns, they become a choice every time they succumb to them. When someone says they have no choice, it's equivalent to them not being accountable for their life. Habits are only beyond the realm of choice when you don't see them; if you see them and can't stop, then you need to come to terms with *why*.

If you see that you're restricted by habits that aren't benefiting you then ask yourself, why? If it's a drug habit, for example, bring into focus the beliefs you've bought into about yourself in *relation* to the substance. Why do you believe you can't live without it? What beliefs are convincing you to kill yourself slowly? Do you believe dying is a better alternative than healing?

Once you make those unconscious processes, conscious, you'll most likely find them to be to the detriment of your self-empowerment. People generally only become addicted to substances (if not for medical reasons) when they believe they need a substitute for their joy which is, in a fundamental sense, their connection to the source within.

When a person desires something, all they're after is the feeling that arises when their desire comes to fulfilment. When you know how to self-regulate your heart centre, however, you're capable of generating bliss and joy independent of outer circumstances. People waste away most of their lives chasing a feeling they believe they can only find in the external world when they already have it within themselves.

The bliss of the divine is an intoxication that surpasses anything drugs or alcohol could give you, and it is *free*, innate to the depths of your own being. Christ said you can't put new wine into old wineskins, and this is what he meant; you can't create a new life from an old state of being. Making your state of being your priority is the *key* to transformation. How liberating it is to know that paradise isn't in the sky, but within our hearts, here, now!

There's a lesson in every experience. Many differentiate between a lesson and a blessing, but for me, lessons *are* blessings as they enable us to expand beyond our limitations into higher states of consciousness.

"Choice not chance determines your destiny."
– Aristotle

We must always be aware of our state of being. When we flow with the guidance of our higher self rather than follow the impulses of the old self, we come into harmony with life. Many of the beliefs installed in the mind attempt to pull you in a thousand and one directions, most of which are usually primrose paths that *leadeth to destruction*. As I said in the previous chapter, a calm mind makes the right decisions. It would be wise to only make decisions from a peaceful state. Choosing out of anxiety is to pick out of fear, and if you're feeling fear, then you're probably misaligned.

CHRIST/KRISHNA CONSCIOUSNESS

Christ consciousness is a concept mentioned in numerous metaphysical works, but what is it? It is simply one's natural state of consciousness, realised when one has found the intricate balance between the ego and the higher self. This divine state is the result of using the mind for its intended purpose, which is to focus you in the present moment, allowing the intuition of the higher self to guide you through the *labyrinth* of timelines that come your way in life.

Why has this state been correlated with beings such as Jesus, Krishna and Buddha? Buddha wasn't Buddha's name: he was *Siddhartha Gautama*. Krishna belonged to the *Yadava* clan, and Jesus was *Yeshua Ben Joseph*. The titles of Christ, Krishna, and Buddha are spiritual titles that emphasise their state of consciousness while they roamed the earth. They manifested divine grace, and the people of their times saw their true selves in them. In eastern traditions, it's common for enlightened masters to hold such titles.

Christ consciousness is a state where you embrace the unknown with such faith that you thrive in it. You go beyond likes and dislikes and act when you need to without expectation. In this state, you trust that each moment in life is sufficient unto itself.

"Forget about likes and dislikes. They are of no consequence. Just do what must be done. This may not be happiness, but it is greatness."
—*George Bernard Shaw*

The present moment is the key to Christ consciousness. When one is present, their personality dissolves; they realise that they're much more than a bunch of likes, dislikes, memories, thoughts and emotions. They become pure consciousness and recognise that their true self is unconditioned by the illusions of the past; forever anew in the still-waters of the here and now.

As a result of going beyond linear space-time, one begins to feel their awareness expanding *beyond* the limited confines of their body. They start to feel the emotions of others they know on the other side of the world and have the same thoughts as them at the same time. This experience can be confusing if you're not centred, but, remember this; if you're capable of feeling the same way as people you know, then you may be operating on the same frequency as them. It isn't always the case, but it could mean that you have the same perceptions as them as your states are identical.

Countless people in spiritual communities believe their turbulent emotions solely belong to someone else. As a result of this, they ignore their feelings and wait for them to pass. Shunning responsibility for your state of being, however, will do nothing but reinforce patterns you don't prefer. Ignoring your fears triggers the nervous system to work to your detriment; it is in your best interest to acknowledge the way you feel by accepting your pain.

"Shine like the whole universe is yours."
– Rumi

It's not possible to experience Christ consciousness if your attention is wholly absorbed in personality hypnotised by the illusion of linear time. Such bondage is negative ego-consciousness; it is to be possessed by an inert persona that pretends to be you, even though, in most cases, it is the opposite of who you truly are. Your Christ-like self is beyond linear time; when you embody timelessness, you realise you're one with the collective consciousness.

Surrender is the key to timelessness, and you enter that domain when you drop the belief that your ego has to figure everything out when it doesn't. Life already works; it doesn't need your help, only your cooperation. Act when you must; take the dog for a walk, wash the dishes, do what you need to do at each moment, but do it with a smile on your face; experience life to the *fullest*.

Your inner self exists on a higher vantage point than your ego. It knows what you don't; it can see what you can't see; the unknown is known to the greater thee. When you close your eyes and meditate, watch the stream of thoughts that pass by your awareness. The more you observe the mind, the more you see through its web of lies. The observer is your Christ-self; have you noticed how it is untouched by anything that happens to you?

Your conditioning makes up the foundation for the time-bound persona. When you awaken to a higher level of perception, you begin to separate yourself from it. A split occurs, with your awareness on one side and the impressions of the past on another. You heal this split by integrating the emotions that form the basis of the limitations you believe restrict you.

As a physical being, you'll always have a personality, but when the true self shines through your ego, your persona isn't fixed or inert; it isn't dependent on your memories of the past to give it a sense of continuity. I wrote in an earlier chapter that the true self is fluid like water; *morphing* itself to any situation life pours it in. The example of Lord Krishna's life illustrated this; he was everything life called him to be, a naughty boy in Vrindavan, stealing butter and freeing the cows. As a teenager, he romanced, played the flute, and defeated his evil uncle Kamsa, who killed seven of his brothers. When he grew up and reached adulthood, he became a kingmaker, a fearless warrior, and the hero of the Kurukshetra war.

Krishna experienced the ups and downs of life with a smile on his face; he innately knew that his inner self was untouched by the transitory events surrounding him. His multidimensional persona has many sides; his seven hundred verses in the Gita are capable of enlightening people from all walks of life. Five thousand years since his birth has passed, and people still look up to his perfect example; he was *one* with life itself.

Christ is also your creative power. When an artist is in their creative flow, they feel like they're creating on autopilot; in fact, it doesn't feel like they're doing anything at all. They become a conduit for the wisdom of the divine and observe it working *through* them. Meditative action is effortless; in it, you need nothing to make you feel whole in yourself. In this state, the Christ intelligence is working through you, and I'm not referring to Jesus, the man; I mean the formless intelligence of the universe, which ultimately has no name or personification.

Human beings, since time immemorial, have attached labels, symbols, ideals, and personifications to aspects of the divine so we can relate to it on a human level. As a result of their devotion, God has appeared to the ancients in human form. The plethora of Hindu Gods and Goddesses, for example, are archetypal symbols one can see as God if they prefer to because nothing is outside of the source. If you prefer to believe Jesus is working through you or that he's your higher self, then you can, because, in essence, he is. We're all part of the eternal body of the formless Christ, and it exists *within* us as our individualised soul.

"Christ has no body now but mine. He prays in me, works in me, looks through my eyes, speaks through my words, works through my hands, walks with my feet and loves with my heart."
– *St Teresa of Avila*

Close your eyes and imagine the best version of yourself; how would you think, feel, and behave? What would you be doing? In what ways would you be a conduit for divine grace to enter this world? Imagine how you would look with the light of the divine shining through your eyes. Embracing life as it happens; beyond likes and dislikes, allowing the guidance of the higher self to lead you to the Promised Land. When Christ works *through* you, you trust in divine timing; you become spontaneous, life seems effortless, magical yet simple in every way!

Life is full of surprises; have you noticed that things hardly ever turn out the way we think they will? The will of the divine is often *beyond* the scope of our physical mind's comprehension. The book of Isaiah illustrates this perfectly:

"For my thoughts are not your thoughts, neither are your ways my ways, saith the LORD."
– *Isaiah 55:8*

Krishna, Christ consciousness is the *same* state. You can label it anything you prefer to because the label is just a way for us to relate to the divine on a human level. Jesus is an inspiration to all sincere spiritual aspirants. The term, *Christ consciousness*, is popular among many because of the loving, compassionate example he exhibited during his sojourn on earth.

"For whosoever shall do the will of God, the same is my brother, and my sister, and mother."
– Mark 3:35

Jesus, the man, however, is not the only son of God. He declared many times that we're his brothers and sisters. If that is so, doesn't that make us God's children too? According to Yogananda, the term is a metaphor for Christ/Krishna consciousness. Christ is known as God's only son because all souls are composed of the same essence; one consciousness that has split itself into many. These individualised souls are the sons and daughters of God. Rumi also said: *we're not just a drop of the ocean, but the entire ocean in a drop!*

In the Vedas, Christ consciousness is called *kutastha chaitanya*. The word kutastha means, *that which remains unchanged*, and chaitanya means *consciousness*. Thus, kutastha chaitanya or Christ consciousness is the level of our being that is *untouched* by the transitory world. In truth, the soul is neither in the world, nor of it.

"But as many as received him, to them gave he power to become the sons of God, even to them that believe on his name."
– John 1:12

ISKCON (International Society for Krishna Consciousness) defines Krishna as the Supreme Personality of Godhead. In truth, Krishna is the *only* personality of Godhead as there is only one. The only son of God and The Supreme Personality of Godhead are the same thing; these labels are different ways of interpreting the same cosmic reality.

The divine expresses itself through each soul in a unique way. Lord Krishna is depicted playing the flute for this reason; symbolically speaking, the flute symbolises the human spine with the energy centres or chakras represented by its holes. Allowing Krishna to play through your spine is to become a conduit for the divine to play a song that it can only manifest through you. The words *Bhagavad Gita* literally means *the Song of God*. Krishna opened himself up to the divine wisdom of the universe in that scripture; as I stated before, people are *still* finding refuge in it, five thousand years later.

Those in the fires of their awakening process oscillate between their true self and their old self until they achieve a permanent shift into the ever-new self. This state of being, whether permanently realised or temporarily experienced, can only be embodied when there is no resistance in your mind towards life. You regain your wholeness of being, and the universe becomes your playground. In realising such wholeness, you utilise your creative power to manifest the will of the divine; to bring heaven down to earth.

COMPASSION

What is compassion? The common definition is to put yourself in another's shoes, to see things from their perspective as they go through a challenging situation. In doing this, you naturally feel inclined to support them. While this is a valid definition of compassion, I'd like to add that we must be there for others without pitying them. Feeling sorry for another does nothing but reinforce the victim mentality that's most likely predominant in them. We must *believe* in others, as the universe never presents one with a challenge, they aren't capable of overcoming. We inspire people a lot more when we *believe* in their capacity to overcome the obstacles life throws at them.

Each person is responsible for their choices in life, and like I just mentioned, we *never* attract a circumstance that we're not capable of handling or overcoming. People often struggle more than they need to because they succumb to the negative definitions their unconscious attaches to the present moment. If you're resisting the challenges in your life, then that resistance only makes them more complicated than they would have been if you gracefully accepted them.

Feeling empathy for others is a divine quality, understanding their challenges and seeing the world *through* their eyes is the foundation of compassion. Wallowing in their misery with them, however, won't help them in any way. We must be a shining example of the divine qualities present within ourselves, because if another can recognise them in you, then it means those qualities also exist in them.

Sympathy isn't to reinforce another's misery by wallowing in it with them; it's a deep understanding of what they're going through. Our true self is unique; no other can replicate it, but we can inspire them to express their own. The only way we can do this is by being the change, we wish to see in the world.

"Our task must be to free ourselves by widening our circle of compassion to embrace all living creatures and the whole of nature and its beauty."
— *Albert Einstein*

When approaching someone who requires your assistance, it's important to remember that they have the right to make their own choices in life. The greatest of healers know that they aren't capable of healing someone without their go-ahead, as one cannot intrude on another's free will. Healers only treat those who believe they can be relieved of their maladies. Even Christ couldn't heal some of the people in his hometown as they never believed in his ability to do so. They had *no idea* who he was; this is because those we grew up around see us for who we were and not who we are in the here and now. When a person breaks free from the illusions of their past and others around them don't, they rarely see the change within them. It's common for people to *project* the negative qualities in themselves onto those who have overcome them. The impressions of their past colour their perception of the present.

"And he said, Verily I say unto you, no prophet is accepted in his own country."
— *Luke 4:24*

Most are doing the best they can, but they simply aren't capable of behaving beyond their current level of development. Yes, there is ignorance all around us; and many aren't aware of themselves. The last thing they need; however, is cold-hearted spiritual people shunning their cries for help in the darkness of physical reality where the illusion of separation from the divine is at its peak. Let us love people with open arms and smile at strangers on the streets. Let's embrace one another as one family, one race, one civilisation because we are one!

Compassion must be the foundation of everyone's spiritual outlook on life. Empathy is the key to transforming society; it is the ability to forgive those who've hurt us by understanding that they have just as much on their plate as we do! Synchronistically, the word compassion has *compass* in it, this is because the state is the compass needle that points us to our true magnetic north, our higher self.

The longest nerve in our body is the *vagus* nerve. The word vagus means *wandering* in Latin. It is known as the wandering nerve as it has multiple branches which diverge from two thick stems rooted in the brainstem and cerebellum that reach down to the lowest viscera of your intestines, touching your heart and most other organs along the way.

Recently, there have been a few studies done to discover the correlations between the vagus nerve and compassion. One study showed a group of students, hooked up to the necessary apparatus, photographs of malnourished children in third world countries. Their vagus nerves exhibited greater arousal the moment they laid their eyes on the pictures, creating more coherence in their brain and body as a result.

Regular activation or arousal of the vagus nerve creates significantly more coherence among the organs of the body. Someone who feels compassion every day, their brain, and heart works in tandem much more than someone who never feels it. Their brain also releases healing chemicals (neuropeptides) from the hypothalamus when they feel elevated emotions such as love, compassion, and inner peace. The results of these findings are conclusive; empathy not only inspires healing in others but you as well! As Buddha once said; if your compassion doesn't include yourself then it is incomplete.

Lynne McTaggart, author of the book, *The Power of Eight*, is the founder of the Intention Masterclass. She connects and trains groups of individuals from around the world in the art of sending their intentions to places where war is predominant and where healing is most desperately needed. McTaggart has found, via her intention experiments that the act of sending healing and loving intentions in groups of at least eight people not only heals those targeted by the group, but it has a transformative effect on the sender's lives as well!

"The outcome of both the groups and the experiments, amazing though they were, paled in comparison to what was happening to the participants. The most powerful effect of group intention, an effect overlooked by virtually every popular book on the subject, was on the intenders themselves."
– Lynne McTaggart, The Power of Eight.

Christ taught that we should love our neighbours as ourselves; this is because our neighbours *are* our self. We are one consciousness, the same spirit occupying different bodies. The separation we perceive with our five senses is strong, but still an illusion fundamentally. As Lynne and others are finding, the best way to heal yourself is to enter the state of self-forgetfulness and focus on loving others. When you become *no-thing*, you merge with all that is.

CONDITIONING

Most of our challenges stem from the process of untangling ourselves from the environmental influences that have surrounded us since we came out of the womb. The majority of people believe that once one is hardwired in a particular way, that they're helplessly stuck, or it is, at the least, extremely difficult to break free from their patterns.

This kind of a mindset is nonsense, however.

Not all change has to be stressful. People make their process more complicated by believing in such ways; their *definition* of change is the issue. The brain is more malleable than we think it is, as we can prune the synaptic connections in our neurology that trigger us to resist life. The goal of spirituality is to become fluid, like water; resembling the chameleon that adapts to its environment by changing its colours.

Thanks to modern technology, we can now study the brain as people are in altered states of consciousness invoked by meditation and other practices. Our neurological makeup is a record of the past; it stores the conditioned persona within its matrix. The lump of meat within your skull is only a dense representation of the neurons that store your personality. The brain is constantly changing; every time you shift a perspective, you alter your neural network into an entirely different version of itself; it's *never* the same.

In this universe of uncertainty, there's only one constant, and that is *change* itself, as everything in creation is transitory. Altering your perception is fundamental to overcoming the limitations you associate with from the illusion of the past. Our perception creates our reality; the filter through which we see things determines how we respond to situations when they arise—every time you tweak your perception, your behaviour, motives, and attitude change.

Also, contrary to popular *belief*, your conditioning is self-imposed on a higher level of consciousness. On a soul level, you chose your society, parents, siblings, and friends. Your patterns are the challenges you've agreed to explore in this life; downloaded into your matrix from the moment of conception—not only from the genes of your parents but also society's influence in moulding you to conform with its ways.

"It is no measure of health to be well adjusted to a profoundly sick society."
― *Jiddu Krishnamurti*

Society is a mixed bag; it isn't all negative. Some of the beliefs and perceptions we acquire from others can also be positive and inspiring. I think it is fair to say, however, that we all grow up with ideas glued to our perception that we don't prefer. In some indigenous cultures, people very much know their worth; they understand that they're an integral component of nature and seamlessly fit in with the earth and all of its flora and fauna. They respect Gaia and cherish her with every step they take on her.

There is a reason why I often define the past as an *illusion*. Physical reality is bound by linear time, which, as Einstein said, only exists to ensure that everything doesn't happen all at once. The *experience* of time, change, movement, progression is a real one; but the mechanics behind it are much different than what we perceive with our senses.

All realities exist now.

What if your *perception* of the past is not only creating your old self but also perpetuating it? If all things exist now, then isn't it fair to say that memories are our way of connecting to an event that is co-existing simultaneously? Many believe their past creates the present, but it is not true; it is their *present* that creates their perception of the past.

Scientists have conducted experiments on memory, and the results were conclusive; in some cases, their test subject's memories were up to fifty-percent incorrect. People make stuff up and believe it to add a sense of continuity to their personality.

Maybe their memories aren't wrong per se; perhaps they changed themselves to such an extent that the person they are now has a different past? In my experience, I recognise that the changes I've made within myself have taken me to a different timeline; altering my past and potential future to align with the version of myself I've become. These multidimensional concepts are difficult to fathom at first, and I can only write from my perspective; what my mind tells me are my past experiences, however, feel anything *but* mine!

This is also why people are experiencing the Mandela Effect a lot more nowadays. Our awareness of multiple timelines is expanding and will continue to do so, not only individually, but also collectively.

As an overview, the fact that we're capable of going beyond our personality proves that it's an illusion. When you see that the continuity of the old self is being perpetuated by your unconscious decision to align with the idea that the past has moulded you, then you'll be able to connect to other versions of yourself. The present moment is your place of power; from this space, you can align with any past or future versions of yourself; cease believing you're limited to just the one between your ears. Be malleable; *fluid*; be whatever life calls you to be!

The above may seem contradictory to your linear time-bound mind but stay with me; we exist on all levels of reality *simultaneously*. The higher self is beyond linear time, while its illusion often deceives the physical mind. From the higher self's perspective, dissolving limiting beliefs is to end your association with timelines, versions of yourself that no longer serve you. Every limiting belief is the product of an experience, and you continue to identify with those events (which you perceive as memories) to give your personality a sense of continuity; but if you've changed timelines, it means you're identifying with someone else's history! From the ego's perspective, this feels like your past has conditioned you and that you're dissolving its influence on your life; looks *can* be deceiving!

CONFUSION

There are two ways to look at any situation in your life; in an expansive or a limiting way. When one feels confused, they define the state as being lost, not understanding where life appears to be taking them. They usually filter confusion through a negative scope, but the truth is, confusing times can be exciting, as they often occur when you're on the verge of learning something.

Embracing the unknown can be bewildering to a mind that loves to organise every little detail of life into compartments to feel safe. Conceptual reality is the very essence of delusion as the true self is beyond the realm of thought and the mind's obsessive need to automatically assign labels onto everything.

When I instruct you to redefine or change the way you look at the situations in your life, I don't mean you should use the same level of mind that triggered you. From a relaxed standpoint, you use your senses to their full capacity to anchor your focus in the present moment, which wipes your windows of perception *clean*; thus, you see things for how they are. The higher self infuses your thoughts with its intelligence when you're in the state to receive it—stillness is vital.

Confusion is a natural aspect of the awakening process; since you've probably bought into countless beliefs that colour your perception, not only of yourself but the world around you. It's normal to experience confusion as you're in the process of rediscovering your true self; not only as a consciousness but as a personality as well.

Contrary to popular belief, we'll always have a personality as physical beings; especially when we interact with others. In solitude, we're capable of transcending the self and becoming pure consciousness, but in our everyday life, we have to play the role as a person and require a persona to do that. Allow the light of the soul to shine through you and not the residue of the past. In life, we must embrace the form and formless simultaneously; be in the world and not of it.

Once you catch a glimpse of the world through a set of unconditioned eyes and then re-identify with the old self; this oscillation can be confusing, but it means you're breaking free from a state of consciousness you've recognised as redundant. Embrace the challenge and learn to enjoy the process.

Challenges push us within ourselves to discover the freedom already built into our consciousness. On the level of the physical mind, when you're confused, it's because you carry two or more conflicting views about a subject, circumstance, or maybe yourself. Confusion is a time when you've unconsciously bought into more than one perspective and are unsure as to which one you should designate as truth. If you're uncertain, rather than choosing with a level of mind that is always in flux, just let it go and allow life to *show* you. Who knows? You may wind up merging both perspectives and develop an entirely new way of looking at things. The universe shows you what it needs to in perfect timing if you trust the direction life takes you, even if the compass needle of your ego is spinning in full circles!

Confusing times are *a process*; be exceedingly patient and allow them to be, because if they've manifested, they are there to show you something important. The universe has a way of revealing answers via the circumstances and synchronicities that appear in your life. When you feel lost, remember that the unknown is *known* to your nonlinear higher self; the truth unveils itself in the end.

"Three things cannot be long hidden: the sun, the moon, and the truth."

– Buddha

Learn to flow with confusion; sometimes it's *better* not to know. We believe we need to know everything, but knowing nothing is, at times, the only way to be shown what is. In the present moment, you live in the state of not knowing; this is known as *the beginner's mind* in the Zen tradition. Open and receptive, you flow with life as if it's a rollercoaster— vulnerable to what it brings you in the here and now. The enlightened ones know how the laws of the universe work and that the present moment is sufficient unto itself.

So, be patient when you're confused; know that it's a process you've created to tweak your perception into what you prefer. Smile in the eye of the storm, and it will smile back. One of the things I admire about Lord Krishna is that he almost always had a smile on his face, even in the most turbulent of times. Live as he did—from your centre, not allowing transitory situations to dictate your state of being.

"He that findeth his life shall lose it: and he that loseth his life for my sake shall find it."
– Matthew 10:39

There are many paradoxes you become aware of when you start to awaken. The Bible and other scriptures are multi-layered; their verses are both literal and metaphorical depending on how you look at them. In the passage above, Jesus is pointing us to one of the great ones. On one level, he's speaking about martyrs and the sacrifice they make for the truth: losing their life for its sake. The deeper meaning of his words is that when one loses their life; the persona they've always defined as themselves, they discover the portable paradise of their true self in their hearts. The Garden of Eden isn't in the sky, but within yourself; how long will you continue banishing yourself from the kingdom of heaven? The gates aren't locked, they are wide open; you just can't find them because your mind has taken you over.

Like everything in life, confusion is a neutral experience; it all depends on how you respond when it arises; so, don't define it in a limiting way. The state usually manifests when you're in the process of finding what's right for you, that doesn't sound so bad, does it?

Learn to lighten up; life can only bring you the answers you seek when you're not in resistance to what the present moment contains. Sometimes, it's necessary to lose your mind to find yourself because it isn't you, and it never was! If you're not at peace, you'll misperceive reality. As the Bhagavad Gita famously says; the tranquil sage goes *beyond* pleasure, pain, praise, or blame. All things serve you if you're in the right state of consciousness, knowing this, you transcend the illusion of duality altogether.

CONTRAST

How many resent their past and live with regrets? Let me assure you; true joy is only a possibility when you've accepted every experience you've had. To resist the past means that it still has some form of control over you.

You integrate experiences by *accepting* them. To resist any aspect of your life is to keep yourself fragmented, and this is what limiting beliefs do; compartmentalise your energy. If you can master the art as seeing all challenges as opportunities for growth, you'll be able to use them as steppingstones to take you to the next level.

There's always a bigger picture, even if you don't see it. You may be in a challenging moment as you read this, and probably have no idea *why* you're going through what you are but let me assure you that you'll know one day. How many times have you looked back and said to yourself, "Ah, so that's why that happened!" In most cases, the circumstances aren't as much of an issue as the way you *perceive* them.

At times, one must conjure up a certain degree of faith by allowing their life to unfold as it needs to. There is only one way a river can flow; you can either go with it or swim against the current, the choice is yours.

Many believe their mind, body and senses are all they are, but if that were so, then synchronicity wouldn't exist, because there is no such thing as coincidences. Everything in your life that has and ever will manifest does so for a *precise* reason.

What level of your being can see the big picture? Not you as an ego, but as the higher self, which is transcendent of linear time. On this level, you can tap into all the potential choices you could make and see their outcome. The higher self is always nudging you in the direction of the path of least resistance, but it can only guide you from an intuitive standpoint. If you're not calm or in harmony with life, then you'll distort its guidance through the scope of your limiting beliefs. Many a time, we crash face-first into brick walls because we refuse to listen to our gut before taking action.

The foundation of all spiritual teaching is to be here *now* because you're only capable of being inspired and guided by the nonlinear aspect of your consciousness when you're at peace in the present moment.

True faith begins to blossom inside of you when you know the roles of the higher self and the physical mind. A lot of the time, people don't trust in the way their life unfolds because their mind has hijacked their consciousness; it attempts to figure everything out on the level of thought. Let me assure you, however, that you're not supposed to figure everything out; how can you embrace the unknown if you already know what's going to happen?

Life loves to surprise us. Have you noticed that when we start obsessing over a specific outcome that it rarely turns out that way? You restrict the higher self by holding onto such ideas. Act, have goals, do what you love for sure, but also be *flexible* enough in yourself to know that if things don't turn out the way you want them to, that it's no biggie, as all circumstances are transitory.

WHAT DOES ALL THIS HAVE TO DO WITH CONTRAST?

Everything, I'll give you an example from my own life to highlight why. I was born in Liverpool in the United Kingdom. As a teenager, those around me influenced me in ways that weren't good for me. Eventually, I was peer pressured into drugs and convinced into believing I was someone I'm not. As my awakening process got underway, it was tempting to keep playing the victim by pointing the finger at everyone else but myself. Instead, I began to take responsibility for all that had happened. I realised that I'd chosen to be born in Liverpool on a higher plane of consciousness, along with the challenges of being a drug addict and gullible enough to buy into everyone's lies. I ended my addiction to intoxicating substances in 2010 and have been clean since thanks to the grace of the divine, but I was still, at first, resisting my past. I subconsciously resented myself. I refused even to acknowledge, never mind *forgive* the past. This resistance prevented me from moving forward with my life.

I will go on record by saying that it's thanks to the contrast that surrounded me during those experiences that you're reading this book. Amazing things happen when you make all experiences, valid chapters in the story of your life. You even begin to *cherish* those dark days, because, without them, you wouldn't be able to see the light of your consciousness shine at its brightest.

Even though from this perspective, the memories do not feel like my own as I have moved to another timeline that's altered my past, my mind tells me they are. Once you reach the point where the past doesn't feel like yours then you've truly healed but there is also nothing wrong with sharing your experiences from other timelines with others to give them inspiration. All experiences in all timelines, through the countless versions of yourself exist simultaneously; own them all as it doesn't matter what happens but what you *make* of it.

Stars can't shine without darkness.

Limiting beliefs are ultimately nothing but *contrast*. The experience of living with illusions hijacking your perception exists to give you a measuring stick; as you have an easier time realising who you are by experiencing who you're not, first. When looked at this way, your past, however dark, serves you. One transcends duality by realising the neutrality of all things; even-mindedness becomes a by-product of doing so. Krishna, in the Gita, pointed this out when he said to his disciple, Arjuna:

"Those who love with the Indestructible, the Indescribable, the Formless, the All-Pervading, the Incomprehensible, the Immutable, the Unmoving, the Ever-Constant; who have controlled their senses, possess Even-mindedness in every situation and devote themselves to the welfare of all beings, truly, I say unto you, they merge into Me!"
– Bhagavad Gita 8:3-4

People need to lighten up on themselves! Your mistakes are simply the contrast you need to better your old self. Make every aspect of your past *valid* and accept your human frailties because you require the challenges that pertain to them on a soul level.

"I form the light, and create darkness: I make peace, and create evil: I the LORD do all these things."

– Isaiah 45:7

Contrast is divine, and in truth, there aren't any dark days in your life, because the moment you see them for what they are, they transform into positive experiences. Connect to the big picture in all experiences by redefining the memories you're resisting between your ears. You'll then extract the hidden lessons that lay dormant, deep below the surface of the so-called darkest days of your life.

CRITICISM

Many in our society immediately reject or take offence to constructive criticism. In some cases, the person doing the criticising may be projecting their issues onto you, but this isn't the issue I want to address here. The *avoidance* of another's criticism, whether true or false, doesn't help you advance in any way, shape or form.

There's nothing inherently negative about a person sharing their opinion of who you are or what you're doing; they're fully entitled to it. More often or not, it says more about them than it does about you, so why not at least *consider* what they're saying? Only when you reflect on another's words are you able to discern whether they are a reflection or a projection.

Most are programmed to judge others according to their past. People, in general, like to feel tall by cutting the heads off others! They're usually quick to criticise people for doing things they're guilty of themselves—this is the definition of *projection*. If you're genuinely coming from a place of love, however, and want to help another become more aware of themselves, then it's fine to offer them some constructive criticism. You must learn the art of speaking when the occasion calls for it by attuning to their feelings and act when the opportunity presents itself.

For example, you may see a habit or belief within someone close to you which they're unknowingly perpetuating. If the person reacts furiously to what you've suggested, then it's likely you have triggered that behaviour in them. When people blow up to your suggestions, it isn't your fault or problem, as their reactions are triggered by them unconsciously allowing your words to define their sense of worth.

The same goes for you. Avoid reacting negatively to anything anyone says about you; to your face or through a third party. Practice responding with awareness, as to *re-spond* is to take *re-sponsibility* for your state of being.

Instead of employing denial, consider what your critic is saying; take their opinion on board. This heightened state of receptivity will accelerate your development. You can then thank them for showing you something you didn't see in yourself if their observation of you is accurate. If what they're saying is incorrect, however, then they're most likely projecting their issues onto you. Don't take it personally, because if you do, then it's triggered your conditioned personality. If their words trigger you, acknowledge your emotions and ask yourself:

"Why has their suggestion triggered me? What beliefs are these feelings showing me? Do I believe what they're saying is true?

Take note of any limiting beliefs you find and reverse them by realising their illogicality and then embody appreciation to the universe for revealing to you more of your old self.

Your state of being is your responsibility and no one else's. Every time you're triggered by the actions of another aimed toward you or someone close to you, then you must, on some level, be buying into what they're attempting to convince you. The truth is that nothing can trigger us; we trigger ourselves by resisting the stimuli perceived through the senses. Aggressive reactions represent your lack of inclination to take responsibility for your state of being as well as your propensity to project the blame onto others; they are a form of denial. Most live in denial because the truth can be a hard pill to swallow.

Have *compassion* for your critics; everyone has their challenges in life and, in some cases, it's better to remain silent; it depends on the person. If the situation is calm and you feel the recipient would heed your advice, tell them they may be seeing themselves in you. It is better to remain silent to the criticism of angry people; they'll see what they're meant to when they're ready.

"The unexamined life is not worth living."
— ***Socrates.***

So, define criticism positively, because if used correctly, it can help you uncover more of the residue that prevents you from expressing your authentic self. Respond *positively*; dare to listen to the criticisms of others and work on bettering yourself whenever necessary. We should be striving to become more of our true selves every day. What is the harm, then, in another revealing to you the elements within you that aren't representative of your truth? Work with criticism rather than against it, and you'll unravel more of the falsity cocooned around you. Every time you receive constructive criticism, it's an opportunity to observe your thoughts and feelings to see if you're holding onto anything you may have picked up from the past; criticism is a great reflective tool, use it; *don't* abuse it.

CRYING

Most males in our society have been conditioned from an early age to believe that expressing emotional pain is a sign of weakness. Teenage boys, for example, make fun of another in their gang if they show their distress by crying. In response to this, to avoid the shame, they feel when their mates taunt them, they resort to anger, fighting, sex, drugs, or alcohol to suppress their grief. This dynamic is one of society's many flaws, but we *don't* have to continue accepting it as normal.

Crying is strength, and whether you cry alone or in front of others, it's better to release the energy in the most natural way. Crying is a mechanism built into the body, and it is there for an important reason. Let's say, for example, that a man is heartbroken because his wife left him for someone else. If he were to show no emotion towards this situation even though he's severely wounded, the pain would break-down, not only his mind but his body too.

Holding onto trauma in your emotional body is detrimental to your wellbeing and is known to be the cause of many illnesses. Scientists have even found that the overindulgence in stress hormones is a cause of cancer and other diseases. Fear-based beliefs generate trauma because they convince us to define ourselves as a victim to circumstances.

The man who lost his wife to another will probably define himself in a degrading fashion due to this experience. His pain will distort his perception, convincing him that he's unworthy. As a result of believing he's unworthy, he'll compare himself to his ex-wife's new man. If he sits down and feels the pain generated by this set of circumstances, it will help him release this pain. The only way out of grief is to go through it; emotions are simply energy in motion, once you accept them, they dissolve.

When we cry, we evaluate our life. We can have realisations about how we've been living up to that point. Crying can trigger changes; it's a healing mechanism not only for the body but also the mind. If you need to cry, then use it to your advantage, but cry with awareness. Be the *watcher*; allow your body to cry as you identify with the deeper aspect of your consciousness that is untouched by transitory circumstances. In this state, you'll see the best path to take and learn things much faster. You'll also release the trauma in your body and feel much lighter when you do.

Befriend your pain, and cry without shame when you need to because it's an outlet designed to *release* you from physical, mental, and emotional trauma.

Tears of joy are even more powerful, cry for positive reasons. Cry in gratitude, in appreciation for who and what you are; a child of the infinite, indestructible, and infinitely loved. When you cry tears of joy, you literally, reinforce your faith and release the toxins akin to your fear-based beliefs in the process.

Many cry when things appear to be going wrong, but it's rare for a person to cry when things are going right. They don't realise how much of a miracle their existence is; they've become accustomed to taking the simple things in life for granted. The fact you exist in a physical body is such a blessing. Too often, we throw the gift of life back into the creator's face when we forget this. Most people are locked in a tunnel vision that focuses on what they don't have or how others have wrong done them. It's essential to focus on what you already have; if you don't appreciate what you have, why would life give you anything more?

Shed tears in appreciation for the simple things in life. Allow the light of the sunrise to pull those tears out of you. Let the stars, the moon, and the sound of a kitten crying to pull those disempowering beliefs out of your body. Joy is all around us, but we don't see it because our beliefs place a blindfold over our eyes. Remove that blindfold to see the love of the source projected all throughout nature; when you do this, you'll transform your life from a nightmare into a lightmare.

DESIRE

The concept of desire has been misunderstood by many religious, philosophical, and spiritual communities throughout the ages. Many eastern faiths teach you to drop all your desires but let me tell you that it was your desires which brought you to this world in the first place.

The power of desire is natural and built into the human condition. The desire to do good and uplift society, for example, can benefit those around us.

The awakened soul is one who has found a balance between the physical mind and the higher self; thus, he knows that his heart's desires will come to fruition in perfect timing. All the experiences relevant to his karmic blueprint will find their way to him if he *trusts* the way his life unfolds.

Our heart's desires reflect the karma we chose before entering this world on a soul level. The things you love and are passionate about are no accident; they *lead* you to your purpose.

Emotional states such as desperation, lack and neediness, send a signal out into the universe that you don't believe you have what you need; this keeps your dreams at arm's length. The man anchored in wisdom knows that there is a perfect time for everything, and that the universe supports him in all his endeavours; even if he chooses to believe he *isn't* supported. Linear time is an illusion, and in a sense, you already have everything you desire, so it's time to start behaving as if you do.

"Therefore, I say unto you, what things so ever ye desire, when ye pray, believe that ye receive them, and ye shall have them."

– Mark 11:24

Our beliefs are the creative seeds which, along with our karma, are the origin of the circumstances we manifest in physical reality. What we believe at any given moment determines where our motivations lie, because we *always* feel motivated to go in the direction, we believe serves us best. Beliefs fuel our behaviour and forge our wishes and desires.

If you have limiting beliefs controlling your perception on an unconscious level, then you'll have many desires that don't reflect the integrity of your soul. You'll feel the urge to do things you *believe* are in your best interest when they aren't.

Let's say, for example, you're single and believe you need a romantic relationship to feel whole. Instead of searching for a partner for genuine reasons, you look out of desperation and end up attracting someone equally as desperate. Your motivations upon entering the relationship weren't pure; they were, rather, the act of using another to fill the void you feel inside you because you believe you're incomplete. This illusion is twofold, however; no one can make you feel whole within yourself, and you're whole already, you just believe the opposite.

So, what is the *source* of your desires? Go to their root to discover the motivations generating them. Do they come from a place of wholeness, harmony, and peace, or are they fuelled by insecurities, neediness, and the belief that you don't already have everything you need? If the latter is the case, then investigate your perception; ask yourself:

"Why do I believe I need this?"

Once you identify the underlying beliefs, you'll see that they stem from a devaluation of your connection to the source. If you don't prefer to buy into these beliefs anymore, then you'll be more capable of releasing them when you realise how nonsensical they are. You can't continue to buy into something you *see* simply isn't true.

These ideas came from the minds of others; they belong to those who raised you and spent the most time with you while you were growing up; *drop* them. Readjust your perception; bring yourself back into alignment.

You transform limitation into freedom by dissolving limiting belief systems. As you do this, your motivations and desires also change. It would be best if you didn't fight yourself; *playfully* work with your resistance; don't take it so seriously. Define the process as a game that you're playing with yourself.

Cease making enemies of your negative thoughts, feelings, and beliefs; they exist to give you contrast, which enables you to perceive the light of your soul more clearly. Work *with* it; befriend your fear-based beliefs, delusional thoughts, and your painful feelings. Define them as messengers that show you the aspects of yourself that you've yet to accept. Once you use the contrast for its intended purpose, it dissolves.

Contrast only bothers people when they resist what it's showing them; thus, they attempt to suppress it. If everything in your reality is created by your essence; however, you can't push anything away as it has nowhere to go other than to return to its source, which is *you*! Embrace the contrast in a playful spirit, and it will serve you. Fear is an illusion that dissolves the moment you face it.

"Just as the purpose of eating is to satisfy hunger, not greed, so the sex instinct is designed for the propagation of the species according to natural law, never for the kindling of insatiable longings," he said. "Destroy wrong desires now; otherwise they will follow you after the astral body is torn from its physical casing. Even when the flesh is weak, the mind should be constantly resistant. If temptation assails you with cruel force, overcome it by impersonal analysis and indomitable will. Every natural passion can be mastered."

– Sri Yukteswar (Autobiography of a Yogi)

Many masters have instructed against chasing your desires, which is understandable because once you know that everything you desire will find you in perfect timing, then there is no need to chase anything. You can have pure desires; however, the key is to develop the *discernment* to identify their source. When you know they are in alignment with the blueprint of your soul then you can set the right intentions, take the appropriate course of action, and allow the higher self to bring them to you in a way that your reasoning mind cannot comprehend.

The soul has desires built into its matrix; your job, as an ego, is to focus your consciousness in the present moment. Leave all important decision making to your higher self, which speaks to you through your intuition. Act when called upon and flow with whatever outcomes manifest in the present as a result of those actions. The higher self brings you what you need, every moment, without fail; even situations to show you that you're *not* listening to it!

Circumstances manifest in your life for one of two reasons; to give you more contrast or to reinforce the bliss of your soul. Indeed, *do* fulfil the desires that are akin to your heart and not from the minds of others. Listen to the yearnings of your inner child; you have them for a reason, fly high in the sky with the wings the divine gave you; it's your birthright!

Many chase mundane desires spawned by illusory beliefs with the expectation that their fulfilment will provide them with the satisfaction they crave. There's nothing inherently wrong in this, as it does bestow much worldly experience and provides you with even more contrast to realise what you truly prefer. You encounter life on both sides of the spectrum, the ups, downs, the pleasures, and pains. It is not my intention to belittle this or claim what is right or wrong. Only when you grow sick of chasing, though, do you realise that you already have *everything*, you need. The treasure was in you all along, but you couldn't see it because your focus was solely on the outer world. The moment you shift your focus and start looking inward for answers, you discover a goldmine.

When speaking of desire, the only real question is; are you controlling your desires, or are they controlling you? When you chase anything to fill a void, you imagine is within you; when false perceptions of incompleteness spawn your desires, then they are controlling you. When you realise that you're already whole, then you can play with the world without attachment. You explore life with a childlike innocence; it will seem like a game to you and not the desperate struggle which convinces people to take every aspect of their lives far too seriously. Control the whims of the old self, or they will control your life.

When you realise that your wholeness of being was there all along, you'll cease allowing the ups and downs of life to define who you know you are at your core.

DESTINY

What is destiny? Is it a valid concept? If we create our reality, then how can we have a destiny? I hear this question often, mainly because many misunderstand the concept of fate.

We, as souls, come into this life having made certain agreements with the collective consciousness in which we have chosen to partake. Karmic themes vary from person to person; the drug addict, someone born with bipolar disorder, the priest, a teacher, or a musician, for example, *chose* these experiences on a higher level of consciousness. Some of the events and conditions in our lives are predetermined. However, there's still a great degree of freedom within this karmic arrangement as they can manifest in a variety of ways depending upon the timeline, you're on.

The talents we're born with and develop as we mature, for example, are no accident. We possess these abilities because we need them to fulfil our purpose, which is to utilise them to serve our civilisation in the most uplifting ways we can. You, as an ego, get to choose how you'll experience the themes in your life, and it's also you who determines whether you'll overcome the challenges that pertain to them or not. Even some of the people we meet at certain periods in our lives; we do so by *agreement*. Soulmates exist, and they come into our lives to reflect certain aspects of ourselves to us as soon as we're ready to receive them. Is this destiny? It is, but there's another side of this concept that requires further clarification.

Many who have fear-based beliefs hijacking their perception define the contrast they attract as a result of buying into those beliefs as their destiny. This is not their destiny, however, but a lack of awareness on their part. To truly experience our destiny, we need to make the darkness in us conscious; otherwise, we end up sabotaging our experience by rejecting the guidance of the higher self.

One's karmic lessons and the people who've had a profound impact on their lives are their destiny, but most *prolong* their obstacles by remaining in denial of them. Predetermined events make their way to you in divine timing, but there are a variety of ways they can materialise. The key is to cease trying to control your life through the scope of your fear-based beliefs and stop seeking joy in things that aren't in your soul's blueprint. Allow life to flow *through* you by embracing the unknown; this will allow your destiny to work its way towards you. The only thing that is keeping your dreams at arm's length is you; learn to get out your own way.

"Until you make the unconscious conscious, it will direct your life and you will call it fate."
– Carl Jung

All things that are meant for us are trying to find their way to us. We repel them, however, when we hold onto false notions about ourselves, exhausting most of our energy by believing we're someone we're not. Once we enlighten the cave of our unconscious by shining our conscious awareness into it, we discover our true self, playing hide and seek behind the cobwebs of our deepest fears.

DISASSOCIATION

Many disconnect from their emotions without even realising, they do this to avoid the pain in their emotional body. If one is to be healed and free from their past, however, then they need to cease trying to avoid their pain, first and foremost.

The words of spiritual masters are often misinterpreted by those who lack the depth to perceive the subtle messages encoded within them. When the masters instruct against identifying with your thoughts or emotions, they don't intend for you to disassociate by suppressing them. Many continue doing this, however, believing they are practising some form of yoga when all they're accomplishing is the denial of their pain. The witness state is not passive; it's intended for you to watch the mind with awareness so that you, eventually, become *familiar* with its patterns.

"Know thyself…"

During the awakening process, it's essential to experience all the perspectives of your conditioning, so they can give you the contrast you need to see through their falsehoods. You're more capable of perceiving the truth by becoming *conscious* of the lies in your brain and body. Ignoring your fears not only creates more chaos and havoc in your brain and mind but also breaks the body down. To ignore is to deny, and how can you heal something that you refuse to acknowledge?

The masters teach that our thoughts and emotions aren't who we are at our core. The automatic ramblings of the mind many allow to define them reflect the collective unconscious. They are merely the residue of your experiences in society with the people you grew up around. You can only embody the true self in the present moment, as the illusions of the past have no power over you when you accept it as it is. Yogananda defined God as *Satchidananda*: ever-existing, ever-conscious, ever-new bliss for this reason.

Consciousness exists on many levels beyond the mind. Your thoughts and emotions, which are generated by your beliefs, are transitory. The true self never changes; it is the kutastha chaitanya mentioned in the Vedic texts; *'that which remains unchanged'*. Christ likened this unchangeable core to a house built on a steady foundation in the Sermon on the Mount. In becoming conscious of your connection to the source by immersing yourself in the present, you discover not only your worth but also your timeless identity:

"Therefore, whosoever heareth these sayings of mine, and doeth them, I will liken him unto a wise man, which built his house upon a rock: And the rain descended, and the floods came, and the winds blew, and beat upon that house; and it fell not: for it was founded upon a rock. And every one that heareth these sayings of mine, and doeth them not, shall be likened unto a foolish man, which built his house upon the sand: And the rain descended, and the floods came, and the winds blew, and beat upon that house; and it fell: and great was the fall of it."

– Matthew 7:24

Most of your thoughts aren't even relevant to who you are in the here and now. If you believe them, you allow them to define you, and when they do, you perceive the present moment *through* the scope of a timeline that may not even be yours anymore. However, whether the experiences are yours or not doesn't matter, as they affect your biology the same, because you seek yourself in them by allowing them to define you.

Becoming conscious of the winds of madness inside you is the key to preventing you from unconsciously disassociating from emotional pain. On the level of thought, take note of any thoughts that contradict each other; this will enable you to see their unreliability. Also, be mindful of the thoughts that have been in your head for years, resembling a tape recorder that repeats itself at random. If your thoughts trigger negative feelings in your body, then it's time to investigate your emotions to find the beliefs reinforcing themselves through your acceptance of them.

Feelings are more challenging to manage, but many of them are ultimately illusions as well. Emotions reflect your perception of your environment. If you're feeling fear, for example, then you must believe you're under some form of threat. Many of your feelings lie to you about your true nature, but even the lies can be great teachers if you use them as a contrast to *discern* what's true for you. Acknowledging fear is the key to dissolving the beliefs generating it. To ignore or to be in denial of your worries is to allow the limiting beliefs to continue hijacking your perception.

Fear is your friend; it exists to lead you to the lies that give the old self a sense of continuity, but it won't be your friend if you continue to ignore it. At whatever rate you're comfortable, dredge into your fear to discover the perceptions causing it. This method is the opposite of disassociation; it is the process of accepting your emotions to listen to what they are telling you. In doing this, you integrate the jigsaw pieces from the puzzle of your being back into its core. You must work with and acknowledge the pain, however, to see it for what it is.

In all healing systems, acceptance is the first step; even in twelve-step programs for alcoholics, they must first accept and acknowledge that they have a problem. Denial is one of the many tools the old self uses to perpetuate its false identity and prevents you from realising your full potential. Any unconscious perception you find that isn't reflective of your integrity *can* be changed; knowing this will make their acceptance easier.

Everyone has the truth hidden within them, and this is why many disassociate from the lies; they subconsciously *recognise* that the negativity in their mind isn't truly representative of themselves but make no effort to face it. If you prioritise a life of health and wellbeing, however, making the unconscious, conscious is *essential*.

EGO

The ego is one of the most complex subjects in this book due to the various definitions of the word. I'd like to start by pointing out that what many believe is their ego, isn't, but an entity they think they need to be in order to fit in with society.

At the most fundamental level of our beings, we're all projections of the same consciousness; we are one, in this sense. The ego exists for a divine purpose. Let's accept our oneness as a fact so we can thrive in our God-given individuality simultaneously. We have our individuality for a reason: without it, we wouldn't exist, period.

Fighting the ego creates an internal split within you as adopting such an attitude is to be in denial of your physical self. Like I mentioned earlier, without an ego, you wouldn't be capable of having the experience of relating to another. To interact with others, you need to appear as separate from them.

The ego and the mind are inseparable; the various levels within the mind consist of unconscious beliefs, subconscious emotions, thoughts, and habits, along with the perceptions of the conscious mind. Rejecting your individuality doesn't benefit you in any way, shape or form. You *can* be aware of your connection to the source while simultaneously thriving in your ego. You'll always have an individual perspective as a physical, astral or causal being, with this in mind, opposing your individuality is illogical; why *negate* the gift of your existence?

You're a piece of coal, plunge yourself into the fires of the infinite spirit and become a diamond, but even a diamond shines on its own. There's no other possibility; you'll always appear as separate from the collective in one form or another. Even when you ascend to the level of consciousness where you *know* the separation is an illusion, you'll still have a unique perspective—an individual focus. The divine sees existence *through* your eyes in a way that it can't through any other.

In my experience, the spiritual path isn't about killing the ego; I've found it to be quite the opposite. True spirituality is the purification and refinement of the ego, enabling it to expand into infinity. When a guitar is out of tune, the musician doesn't smash it over a table to destroy it; they *retune* the instrument, so it correctly expresses their creativity as they play it. Similarly, we must *fine-tune* ourselves to become instruments for the divine consciousness.

The soul is untouched by the world of form; it is the witness, observing all situations from a transcendent perspective; dreaming this life from the realm of oneness in the source. The old self (what many define as ego), is fabricated by our experiences in the outer world. The wisdom of the higher consciousness is filtered *through* the beliefs in the old self, which often misinterprets it.

From a tender age, the people around us; mainly those who raised, befriended, or taught us in school, condition us to conform to their ways. Almost everyone in our lives has had their share in fabricating the old self, which obstructs the full expression of the true self. Our conditioning doesn't have to be defined negatively, however, as it provides us with the contrast that enables us to perceive our true nature. Society is a mixed bag; it isn't all negative—some of the beliefs and values your loved ones teach you are wonderful and should be passed onto your children if you have them. In most cases, though, people inherit a tonne of negativity and have no idea how to dissolve it.

Most of the things we believe about ourselves and the world around us are false notions we've bought into via our interactions with others. Such conformity is the opposite of individuality, yet many define our conditioning as our ego; do see the contradiction? The true ego has *nothing* to do with who other people believe we should be.

The ego is divine; the conditioning is not the true ego; it's the person you believe you need to be to gain social acceptance. At Christmas, you put decorations on your tree to make it look all Christmassy; but the tinsel, coloured balls and bells aren't the tree. It is the same with us; the personality is merely a bundle of decorations on the tree of our ego, which consists of likes, dislikes, beliefs, definitions, attitudes, memories (identification with simultaneous existing events which give our persona continuity) and habits.

On a physical level, an ego is required to focus you in the present moment; that is why it's synonymous with the senses. When you're fully present, do you notice that your personality dissolves, even if only temporarily? This state is your true self, but as you're in it, you still have an individual focus; your individuality is your ego, and it's a beautiful thing.

Many are indecisive because their mind is full of ideas that compartmentalise their energy. We create much turmoil for ourselves when we allow false expectations and assumptions that stem from the old self to influence how we believe life *should* unfold. It would benefit us to drop these notions and allow life to work for us by embracing the unknown.

So, you don't kill the ego; you *refine* it by dissolving its lies. The spiritual path is the process of dissolving the old self via introspection and meditation. Spiritual awakening is an alchemical process, as waves of the residual baggage periodically surface to be dissolved.

Enlightenment is the by-product of two things; becoming childlike, by lightening up on yourself and dissolving the lies that are cocooned around your consciousness. At daytime, you can't see the stars in the sky, but that doesn't mean they aren't there. Similarly, just because you don't know how to access your true self, doesn't mean that it isn't there.

"And said, Verily I say unto you, except ye be converted, and become as little children, ye shall not enter into the kingdom of heaven."

– Matthew 18:3

Yogananda, the Hindu master who lectured all over the United States in the early 20th century often spoke of the divine ego, and this is what he meant. In the ultimate sense, the ego is the soul itself, as individualised souls are wrapped in causal bodies to give them the illusion of a separate existence. The ego exists on all three levels of reality: physical, astral, and mental (causal), with the latter being the closest to the source.

The ego is a blank canvas, every moment, but we give our persona continuity by identifying with a collection of memories. Through this unconscious process, people limit themselves to just one rigid personality structure; but what if you could become like water? The true self is fluid and *morphs* itself to every situation that arises when it expresses itself through the physical ego. Lord Krishna lived this truth beautifully; he had so many dimensions, which often confused his onlookers. Don't be stiff; be malleable, be whatever life calls you to be.

"I protest by your rejoicing which I have in Christ Jesus our Lord (Christ consciousness), I die daily."
– Corinthians 15:31

As one is in the process of dissolving the elements that make up the old self, it can almost feel like they're dying. They've defined the false beliefs and perceptions as themselves for so long that even just a couple minutes of living in the present triggers their fight or flight response, which defines the unknown as uncharted territory, thus a *threat*. It is like a bird which has been locked inside a small cage for years. Once you open the door, it will feel reluctant to leave as it doesn't know anything about life outside of the cage. At first, it may examine near the door, then take a foot outside and jump back in. Eventually, it will begin to feel comfortable outside and use its wings to soar into freedom!

"Why do you stay in prison when the door is so wide open?"

—Rumi

You also have wings; you've just forgotten how to use them. Don't fight against the gift of your existence; embrace it! Not all illusions are negative; in many of the spiritual traditions, there are limiting beliefs about these ideas, which aren't very practical. Refine your ego and *thrive* in it.

EMOTIONS

Emotions are an essential part of our experience of life. Our feelings are important to us, as we use them to express ourselves. I've met a few people who believe that sensitivity is a weakness, as opposed to spiritual seekers who claim that they're able to go beyond their emotions without being directly influenced by them. The issue is that many who believe they're controlling their emotions are suppressing them. They think they've healed their pain but have repressed it to such an extent that it feels like it isn't there. If not integrated, pain always returns, and usually when we're least expecting it; resembling a volcano that erupts after being inactive for centuries.

Emotional intelligence is something that only comes when you *surrender* to them. Mastery of your feelings requires you to be aware of yourself on many different levels simultaneously to clear yourself out of the baggage that keeps you chained to the illusions of the past.

Once you stop resisting your emotions, you'll realise that many of them are deceptive in nature, which means your feelings can be as unreliable as your thoughts.

Every emotion a person feels is triggered by what they believe, on some level, to be true. If they're feeling fear, then there must be an underlying belief they've bought into generating it. Think about it; if the stress response is activated in the body, they must *believe* they're in some form of danger. Excluding a life-or-death situation, they only do so when their perception is misaligned.

Please contemplate on this for a moment.

Look at any situation in your life or any so-called, past time spinning on the carousel of your mind. You need to realise that it's not the memories that generates the feelings you experience when you think of them, but the *scope* you filter them through.

An excellent method of untangling yourself from the past is to think of any traumatic experience you've had and go into the feelings it generates; *allow* it to trigger you as it usually does. What do you believe is true about yourself because of that situation? Do you see the definitions you've unconsciously assigned to the experience? Maybe you see yourself as a victim? If this is the case, then change the way you look at it. You can't change what has happened in *that* timeline, but you can change the way you look at it. Paradoxically, when you change how you look at what's happened, you render a completely different effect from the situation; thus, a new experience has been born through the new scope you perceive it through.

Nothing happens by chance; everything has a specific reason for manifesting in our life. Whether it's a harmonious or challenging experience you're presently dealing with, it's essential to keep a positive attitude and look on the bright side. In keeping a positive and even minded attitude towards all the circumstances that manifest, you go beyond duality; thus, your development accelerates tenfold. Remember now, that it isn't what happens, but what you do with it that counts; all circumstances are neutral until you define them.

Instead of succumbing to automatic, fear-based definitions and thus, experience only resistance and struggle, focus on the exciting challenges life has placed before you. Don't play the role of the unconscious victim by wallowing on what's happened to you. Focus, instead, on what the experiences *taught* you about yourself and life as a whole. Accept the experiences gracefully as if you've chosen them because, in reality, you have. Even when you're not in harmony with existence, you're pushed back into alignment by challenging situations.

> *"Nothing happens to man without the permission of God."*
> *– Euripides*

So, whether it's a memory or the circumstance at hand; your definition determines the way you feel about them as they are all neutral, initially. As you become watchful of the mind's processes, you'll see its habit of automatically defining circumstances negatively and how those unconscious definitions colour your perception of what is. Becoming aware of these automatic filters enables you to go back to neutral; in a state of still-acceptance of what the present moment contains. When you still the winds of madness between your ears, your higher consciousness can use what's happening to your benefit.

Working with negative emotions generated by automatic definitions is essential. Validating darkness instead of resisting it, transmutes the contrast to create more space in you. The more space there is in you, the brighter you can shine. Unacknowledged pain stored in your body creates a host of energetic blockages within your spinal centres—the alchemical process of transforming the darkness of your emotional pain into light is the goal of the spiritual journey. You progressively feel *lighter* with the more pain you transmute because it's only the negativity stored in your body that weighs you down.

We must feel our pain to be free of it, but don't worry, feeling it won't kill you; it will only kill what *isn't*. As I stated before, a large percentage of people claim that it's a weakness to feel any sort of emotional pain, but the opposite is true, in my opinion. Running from your fears and suppressing emotional pain is known to be the causes of both physical and psychological illnesses. Suppressed emotional pain is the reason why so many are unwell. Genes may also be a factor but even science, over the last few decades, has discovered that changing our perception of life has a direct influence in changing our gene expression. Look into *epigenetics*, and the work of Bruce H. Lipton, Ph.D., for more information.

Healing deep-seated emotional wounds can be challenging. Many refuse to face the uncomfortable feelings in their body because they're too afraid to feel their trauma; here is a simple technique to help you transmute your pain if you feel you're ready:

When you feel misaligned, lay flat on your back on your bed using a pillow as a headrest. Close your eyes and stay completely still; don't even move your fingers or toes. Put your focus on the inner energy field of the body; *feel* it from within. As you're lying there, also direct a portion of your awareness on the natural flow of your breathing. As you watch your breath and feel your body, put yourself in total acceptance of what you're feeling and whatever happened to trigger you. Accept the pain you feel *without* resistance; as it's what the present moment contains.

Emotions are transitory; the feeling won't last forever, tell yourself that this too *shall pass*. You must accept all that is happening within and around you to go beyond the pain you're feeling as the powerful flow of acceptance miraculously transmutes all it touches. Your body may even begin to shake as you feel the pain, but don't worry, this too *shall* pass. As the eternal witness, you'll make it.

Lay there for as long as you feel is necessary. This purging of your emotional body is one of the many ways of experiencing a rebirth. Resembling the legendary Phoenix, you'll arise from the ashes of your old self and be born anew. After you change your state of being, you'll feel lighter and even joyous when you stand up; this is because you're no longer in resistance to the emotion. The moment you accept something in life, it stops bothering you. The emotion just wants to be accepted so it can flow without obstruction. That is all the integration of negative beliefs boils down to, overcoming the harmful emotions of the old self.

Any real change happens primarily on the level of *feeling*. All healing happens in the heart centre. Thinking positive thoughts all day but feeling the opposite of those thoughts won't change anything. The subconscious and unconscious minds control 95% of your energy, while the conscious mind only has around 5% to utilise. Learning how to open your heart centre by living in a joyful state on every level of your being is fundamental to inner transformation.

Getting *beyond* the analytical mind is required to penetrate the subconscious, which is only possible when you feel elevated emotions such as love, gratitude, and joy. Most don't know how to generate joy with their eyes open; a consistent practice of transcendental meditation that helps them get beyond the old self can help them in this regard. Once you know how to tap into the portable paradise in your heart with your eyes closed, you'll know how to generate the feeling with them open; then you'll be in paradise all day.

Ultimately, everything in the universe is energy and this energy only becomes positive or negative when it flows through expansive or limiting beliefs in the mind. That is why when you redefine a situation, you once saw as unfavourable into something beneficial, your feelings about the event change. Always be mindful of how you're defining the present moment as the old self will often try to convince you to see it through a fear-based scope.

Intuition is an inner knowing, only possible to tune into when you're calm and relaxed. The higher self speaks to you through your intuitive faculty; through the feelings that arise in the heart. Learn to feel more and think less.

As I have already stated, some of our feelings are extremely deceptive, as you're capable of feeling good about something that isn't good for you or others. One must be self-aware and have a compassionate foundation to their approach to life, not only toward others but also themselves. Our feelings for others are essential to establishing our connection to the divine, as everyone is a valid aspect of it. Empathy is something we should put into practice daily. Feel for others, live for others, and serve them in the best way you can; just don't *neglect* yourself in the process.

EXPECTATIONS

Most have been conditioned from a tender age to be full of fear-based expectations. As a result of this, their mind often expects the worst is going to happen by default; convincing them to often *assume* that something life-threatening is just around the corner, waiting to get them. Expectations are the same as assumptions; if a person persists in believing them, they could potentially crystallise into form in their reality.

In the Bhagavad Gita, one of the main aspects of karma yoga (the yoga of action) is the practice of *Nishkam Karma* or desireless action. This practice is to completely immerse yourself in your activities, so you don't think about its outcome; allowing the result to be what it *needs* to be. When you allow the result to come of its own accord, you're surrendering it to the manifesting power of the higher self, rather than what the old self believes it *should* be. Only in such a state, are your actions free of the selfish motives spawned by the beliefs that convince you to act out of anxiety instead of joy.

"Writing is a good example of self-abandonment. I never completely forget myself except when I am writing, and I am never more completely myself than when I am writing."

– Flannery O'Connor

When a person puts their full awareness and concentration into each action, they become so immersed in its performance that they enter into bliss; this is *meditative* action. To act in such a manner is true selflessness because the identity one has always defined as the *self* dissolves in the state; thus, they become a conduit for divine wisdom. Paradoxically, however, it's only in this state are we anchored in our true nature. We must lose ourselves to discover what we are. Only in the present moment are we capable of acting without reinforcing the selfish motives generated by the beliefs in the unconscious.

"O Best of the Bharata's! Relinquish all activities unto Me! Dropping all egotism and expectations and with your attention focused on the soul, be free from feverish worry, be fully immersed in the battle of right-action!"

– Bhagavad Gita 3:30

Krishna defines the spiritual path as the battle of *right action* because actions speak louder than words; your actions say everything about you. Right action has two aspects; firstly, you should perform the worldly duties aligned with your soul and secondly, the state of consciousness in which you undertake such activities. For example, you can be doing the thing you need to be doing at any given moment, but if you aren't putting all your focus into its performance, then you're still not in the correct state. If there isn't a lightness, playfulness and bliss while doing that which ignites your soul, then you're in your head too much; move into your heart and immerse yourself in the still-waters of the here and now.

Again, we come back to the roles of the physical mind and the higher self. The mind's job is to anchor your consciousness in the present moment, with the higher self taking care of how the fulfilment of your wishes come to fruition. When you desire something, and who doesn't? It would be helpful if you released the fear-based grip the mind has over your reality; surrender the need to know *how* things will come about to the higher self. Let go and allow the divine to bring you the outcomes you need. In the fortress of faith in divine timing, you'll obtain everything you require for your dreams to become a reality.

Your higher self manifested everything that has ever happened to you; even challenging situations appear to shift you back into alignment if you're not heeding its guidance. A certain level of faith is required; *believe* you'll always get what you need in life, because you do if you have the eyes to see. Paradoxically, you *can* expect good things to come your way; it just isn't wise to be too specific. With the knowledge that the higher octave of your being has your back, it will shower the fruits of your optimism gracefully upon you.

Surrendering to the unknown is the only way to live without false expectations sabotaging your experience. Have you noticed that when your mind tries to guess how something will come about that it rarely turns out that way? Life is *full* of surprises. These expectations are defence mechanisms built within the mind to keep its control over reality because it believes it needs to do *all* the work when it doesn't. Give the responsibility of taking care of the how to the higher self and focus your attention on the now.

The key is to first, *notice* and drop the assumptions and expectations your mind automatically assigns to the present moment and return to stillness. Once you can do this consciously, you'll see many of the fallacies hijacking your perception, as they reflect the beliefs relevant to your past experiences. The old self only colours the present through the eyes of the past if you don't have the awareness to see it. Once you can return to neutral, you behold reality for what it is, a *blank* canvas. You'll start to perceive reality through the eyes of the higher self; the *intelligence* of the soul, the aspect of your being that is conscious of your oneness with the source.

FORGIVENESS

Forgiveness isn't a concept that needs *redefining*, but there are deeper levels to this healing act most don't realise. Forgiveness not only has a cleansing effect on ourselves but others too if we're willing to include them in our efforts to make peace with the past.

You'll be more capable of forgiving yourself when you accept, not only who you are, but also every aspect of your past, including all the choices you've made, and the experiences you've had as a result of those choices.

How freeing it is to resist past experiences no longer! Making everything *valid* enables you to move forward with your life. If you struggle to do this, then change the way you look at the memories your mind revisits daily. You achieve this by seeing the experiences you resent for what they taught you instead of reinforcing the victim mentality by focusing solely on how others hurt you.

The vast majority in our society play the victim to the circumstances that arise in their day-to-day lives, even though they aligned with their frequency to bring them into manifestation. This mindset convinces them to see their unpleasant experiences only for what people *did* to them; thus, they remain defined by the illusions of their past. People often dwell on what others did to them through their memories. This wallowing on the past, however, not only distorts their perception of the present but also reinforces the victim mentality currently enslaving billions worldwide. The time is ripe for us, as a collective, to take responsibility for *how* we react to the situations that appear in our lives. We need to be aware of the underlying lessons in every experience we have or are going through because each moment is an opportunity to discover more of ourselves. Once we extract the diamonds from the dark caves of our painful memories, the light of our consciousness shines within them. We then come to see the experiences for what they are and *why* they manifested in our life at that moment through the eyes of the nonlinear higher self, which sees the *big* picture.

All our experiences, past, present, and future are *intertwined*. Something that happened to you ten years ago may end up serving you next week. A lot of the time, and especially during challenging times, it's easy to lose sight of the big picture. All circumstances, however, are *valid* chapters in the story of your life; therefore, it's better to own and acknowledge all the experiences you've had so you can move forward without regret. Nothing goes away until you stop resisting it; to forgive is to *forget*. When you make peace with yourself in regard to a painful memory, you close the connection to the version of yourself in that timeline, and those whose actions convinced you to hurt yourself through your reaction to them.

Changing the way, you look at things, then is the *key* to doing this. I've already said in a previous chapter how changing the way you look at any circumstance, whether in the present or a memory, modifies the effect you get from it. All situations are *neutral* in life; if you have a difficult time releasing experiences, it's because your perception of them doesn't work for you. Look at things in a new light, and you'll learn *new* things. Your perception is power; utilise yours masterfully, and you'll be able to transform your biggest lessons into your biggest blessings.

It is entirely irrational to resent yourself for any mistake you've made. When we make a mistake, and who doesn't? It's because we didn't have the appropriate level of consciousness to realise what we were doing at the time. You can tell when you've genuinely begun to forgive yourself when you can laugh at how unaware you were in the past, as opposed to who you are in the present. Taking the spiritual path too seriously is a colossal net that captures many. You heal when you dissolve this seriousness, which is the foundation of the old self, and express your childlike nature, more often than not.

Laugh at your errors which didn't cause people any harm, you were clueless then, and you're clueless now, as there's always more to unravel. Self-discovery *never* ends; trust in the process and timing you arrive at each level of consciousness; you get to where you need to be, exactly *when* you need to. In a playful spirit, do your best to learn from your mistakes, so you don't have to repeat them.

"Forgiveness is not an occasional act, it is a constant attitude."
– Martin Luther King Jr

Forgiving others not only empowers you but them too, as everyone is fundamentally the same consciousness. Sometimes, when you make peace with another who's hurt you in the past, your mercy and compassion can touch their hearts and trigger changes in them. They no longer reflect the resentment you felt towards them, but your love for yourself and them as well. Christ heroically gazed up at the heavens and screamed as he was nailed to the cross, *"Father, forgive them, for they know not what they do!"* He knew the healing power of forgiveness, and the compassion he displayed during his time on earth is why he's the most well-known historical figure of all time. Jesus walked on water, turned it into wine, and brought back the dead, but his biggest miracle was this—divine mercy to those who didn't know him.

You also don't have to be around another to forgive them. You can do it from a distance if you feel its best, which is necessary sometimes. If you're no longer resentful in your thoughts and wish the best for them, then you've forgiven them inwardly, which is all that matters.

It's natural to forgive, forget and shed the skin of your past, every moment; you just *believe* the opposite. You must unlearn these habits and change the way you perceive the challenges of life to embrace them in their totality. Fear-based beliefs convince you to see an inverted reality, which means you don't see what is, but what *was*.

You must also train yourself not to take the actions of others aimed at you *personally* as they are powerless without your reaction. If you find yourself blowing up and reacting to another's shenanigans, then you most likely, *believe* what they want you to. When you realise that many of the people in your reality are mirrors of your unconscious, however, then you can more easily make peace with them by working with the reflections you're given.

GETTING CREATIVE: BUILDING A FUTURE SELF

The illusion of linear time hypnotises us the moment we come out of the womb. Quantum Physicists are discovering, however, that on the most fundamental level of reality, all things, people, places, realities, events—the entirety of creation co-exists, simultaneously in an invisible field of energy and information—this is the *Quantum Field.*

The darkness we experience behind closed eyes during deep meditation is this field. When meditative practice is executed correctly, we *transcend* our time bound mind, personality, and identification with our mortal coil to go beyond linearity into the non-physical domain. This field isn't experienced with the senses but perceived as an awareness; it is from this place that all conscious creation takes place.

The Quantum Field is the void from which all things in existence arise. Any reality you can conceive of already exists; including all the *versions* of yourself, you can imagine.

"If my mind can conceive it, and my heart can believe it, then I can achieve it."
—*Mohammed Ali*

Many allow their past experiences to define them. Yet, it is only the belief that those experiences are theirs, which keeps them defined by timelines which may not be *relevant* to who they are today. What do I mean? Stay with me here because these multi-dimensional concepts can be challenging to grasp initially.

Every change we make in our inner world is a complete change; we not only change the future, but the past is equally as *malleable*. A true transformation is a shift to another timeline;

where we move to a parallel reality reflective of the new state of being or a version of ourselves, we've become.

I'll give you an example to illustrate my point. My memories tell me that I used to be a drug addict from the age of fourteen to twenty-three. After a spiritual experience in 2010, however, everything changed. I won't go into the details of the experience, but I assure you that I woke up the next day a completely different person. I felt the shift, viscerally. I had new desires, new goals, motivations, but most importantly, I had no cravings for intoxicants. I feel as if I *never* suffered from the addictions in the first place, and the reality is that it's true. In this timeline, I never was a drug addict; even *if* my memories tell me that I was.

Fast forward over a decade later, and I'm still free from those addictions. When I reflect upon the memories between my ears, though, most of them feel like someone else's. The changes that occurred within me were so radical that my memories feel like someone else's experiences, and that's because they are.

However, if we believe the memories between our ears are our own, thus allow experiences from a different timeline to define us, they still affect our brain and biology the same way real experiences do. This is because our perception signals our gene expression. Belief is a powerful force, and for the most part, it is an *unconscious* process within a person until they endeavour to become conscious of what's going on inside them.

Self-awareness is the basis of shadow work, but that is all it is for—to *know thyself*. The Tibetan definition of the word, Meditation, means to become *familiar with*, but familiar with what? The more aware you become of your true self, then the more aware you become of what *isn't* by contrast. Most people are programmed to resist their shadow, and this only reinforces the illusions of the past within them and consequently, keeps them defined by timelines they're no longer on!

The good news is that in the same way one focuses on the past and reinforces tendencies and habits via their association, so too can we focus on the *future* selves we wish to become and prime our brain and body ahead of the experiences relevant to them.

How do we envision a future self?

First and foremost, it's crucial to become *clear on what you want your future to look like*; a clear intention is vital. Once you know what you want, you can imagine being in that timeline, having the experiences that version of yourself is having in the eternal now. It is essential to be as specific and detailed as you can as this creates a *clear intention*. Think of intention as a *blueprint* you're handing over to your higher self. The better the blueprint, the better the non-physical aspect of your consciousness can operate as it has more to work with.

Most keep their dreams at arm's length because they lack *clarity* on what they want, or who they wish to become. So, the first step is to be clear on who you want to be. Changing your mind all the time is the same as handing one blueprint over to the universe, then while the higher self is in the process of building that reality, you tell it to scrap it and hand it another, and another, and another until you've become old a lot faster than you should have because you've allowed the hormones of stress to dictate your life.

If you don't know what you want, then I encourage you to do some soul searching to discover what you're passionate about in life. Follow your passions, and they'll lead you to your purpose.

The next step is to *accept the reality you're in now*. Acceptance is the key to any real, lasting changes because resistance to what you don't prefer only reinforces it in your reality. So, if you have certain tendencies or a living situation, you don't like right now, first of all, acknowledge and accept it. The reality you're in now is the result of your present state of consciousness, and to shift your state you must, first of all, acknowledge and allow the energy of your current state to *flow*. Resistance only blocks the energy; thus, you won't be able to move through what you do not prefer.

After accepting and acknowledging your present reality, it's time to *connect to the future reality*, linearly speaking, of your preference. You can move as far up the timescale as you wish to. You might want to connect with a version of you a year into the future, or five or ten—this is up to you. This process is unique for every person.

Once you know the timescale you wish to connect to, then begin to *build the blueprint of the self* you want to become within that time. Write down or copy and paste the questions below and answer them; this will help you map out a clear intention:

What has your future self achieved what you haven't yet? What do they think and feel daily? What are their passions and excitements? How do they wake up each day? How do they sleep at the end of each day? What is their living situation? How do they treat their loved ones? How do they treat strangers? How do they communicate with others? What are their goals and ambitions? What dreams have they realised? How do they strive for self-improvement daily? What motivates them? What limiting beliefs have they dissolved? What habits have they overcome?

If you can come up with more questions to help you build a vision of your future self, then, by all means, do so. The questions above are just examples; edit them in whatever way serves you best; they are there to help you get a *feel* for the blueprint you wish to create.

Once you've built the model, the next step is to take note of any beliefs or ideas within you that *contradict* your vision. If you have limiting beliefs in your unconscious that make you resist what you want, then your belief in such ideas will only keep your dreams at arm's length. Clearing yourself out of the clutter, at least temporarily, that doesn't align with your vision is essential in this process.

We're at our most creative when we get *beyond* what we've always defined as our personality. In our natural state, there is no person, only pure consciousness. When we become no-thing, we merge with all that is in the Quantum Field; the realm of infinite possibilities. To make ripples in the fabric of space-time, you're going to have to, first and foremost, get beyond what you've always *believed* is your identity and the limiting beliefs that pertain to it. This is where meditation comes into play, as meditation takes you beyond the person and the masks that person wears, into your true, nonlinear nature.

The next step is *visualisation*. Meditate in a dark, quiet space. Disconnect from your outer environment, your body, your senses, become aware of awareness itself in the void of the Quantum Field. In deep stillness, with the blueprint of your clear intention already mapped out, *imagine, envision* what it would be like to be that person. How would it feel? What is their state of being—embody it. What would you experience *as* that person? Envision a scenario as your future self, give it all the sensory perceptions you possibly can in your imagination. For example, if you imagine you're in the best shape of your life, playing five sets of tennis in a years' time, feel the heat of the sun on your face as perspiration drips from your forehead. Feel the tennis ball and racket in your hands as you're about to serve; hear your friend or partner laugh as you ace them! Imagine this from a deep meditative state. After some time of doing this—open your eyes but keep hold of the feeling for as long as you can. *Drop the image!* As the image you visualised is only there to connect you to the state of being of your future self. Once you connect to their state and *become* that version, look out, the synchronicity in your outer world will *reflect* those changes.

One thing I'd like to add is that just because you connect to the future self doesn't mean you won't have to work to have the life they're already living. What connecting does is gives you their mindset, their insight, and inspirations. You see the world *through* their eyes; thus, you'll make better decisions from a higher level of perception. Your work will flow a lot easier, especially creative projects—you'll feel the wisdom of your future self pour *through* you as I do as I write this chapter.

Consistency is *key*. You can't do this once and expect things to change straight away; they might, but it's highly unlikely. Also, the more *energy* you give your future self, then the more you'll dissolve the impressions of the old self. Where you place your attention, your focus is where you place your creative power. Put your attention on a future self, and you'll effortlessly begin to *untangle* yourself from those timelines you've always believed defines you. One day, you'll wake up *as* the future self; ready to conquer the world with joy at your centre.

The steps are as follows. I call them the *Seven Steps to the Kingdom of Heaven.*

1. Get clear on what you want (clear intention) (*Root Chakra*)
2. Accept your present reality (*Sacral Chakra*)

3. Move up the timescale (***Solar Plexus Chakra***)
4. Build the blueprint of your future self (***Heart Chakra***)
5. Become aware of the beliefs that aren't aligned with your vision (***Throat Chakra***)
6. Visualise being your future self, connect to their state of being (***Third Eye Chakra***)
7. Drop the image and keep hold of the state (***Crown Chakra***).

"The clue to the real purpose of life is to surrender yourself to your ideal with such awareness of its reality that you begin to live the life of the ideal and no longer your own life as it was prior to this surrender. "He calleth things that are not seen as though they were, and the unseen becomes seen."

-Neville Goddard: The Power of Awareness

The universe is a library of the countless versions of yourself that you can choose to embody at any given moment. That's how powerful you are at your core. This includes the version or the old self that continuously spins on the carousel of your thinking mind. The moment you *cease* believing in the thoughts that pertain to it, you'll reclaim your freedom and be reborn anew, each moment in the eternal now; the window, to all other versions of yourself.

If you struggle with this process that I've outlined and need assistance, I now do one to one sessions on Skype or Zoom, where I help you build a blueprint of your future self. Visit my website, **www.reirei.co.uk** for more information.

God

God has been one of the most controversial topics since time immemorial; the concept has brought great joy to countless people throughout the ages and much pain to others. The main cause of the suffering is that many *assume* they know what the divine is without any first-hand experience; without it, however, what is their so-called knowing?

Assumptions based solely on religious scriptures.

First of all, in a religious context, how does society define God? Well, that depends on the religion as each has its own way of interpreting God, existence, and our relationship to it. The numerous world religions are all valid ways of connecting to the divine because people have different temperaments; thus, various ways of relating to the source are required. No religion, however, holds exclusivity over truth; some just contain more limitations than others.

Catholics, for example, are taught that God is a Heavenly Father with a white beard, living among the clouds, surrounded by legions of angels blowing their trumpets to glorify him. They believe he watches over his creation, blessing the righteous and judging the sinners. This definition may be valid to those who prefer to buy into this way of thinking, but in truth, it's an outdated way of looking at things. It stems from an age which was plagued by fear, superstitions, limiting beliefs and spiritual ignorance.

Christ defined God as his Heavenly Father, not because God is a man in the clouds, but because the source is the very fabric of the universe which *conceived* us into existence. The issue with this definition is that these people believe the divine is something outside of themselves. Their priests teach them that they're not one with the source, and this way of thinking generates a tremendous amount of suffering because to believe you're not part of the collective is an extremely lonely place to be. Even though in reality, you could never *not* be one with the source, the effects of what we believe are so strong that buying into this belief creates the experience as if you are on the level of feeling. To think you're separate from God is to make yourself an isolated fragment, and no one in the right mind would *consciously* desire to be that!

When the mystics talk about the experience of God, they define the state with words such as bliss, joy, oneness, and unconditional love. These are all excellent words to describe the *experience*, but just reading about it won't enable you to have it for yourself. The experience is one *you* must have, and it will be totally unique for you as your point of view is unique, thus, cannot be replicated by another. Just as no two snowflakes are identical, so too, does every fragment of the infinite consciousness *perceive* itself in a way that is unique unto itself.

On the level of the *macrocosm*, the source is everything, but on the *microcosm*, it is the highest potential for each person. People correlate the divine state with names such as Zen, Buddha Nature, Christ consciousness, etc. These labels are merely invitations; doorways designed to allure you into having the experience for yourself.

Mastering the art of staying present is the key to becoming aware of your connection to the source. The fire of the eternal now burns away the unconscious in you, as it brings up aspects of the old self that don't align with your soul to be integrated. This includes those definitions, through which you've been unconsciously filtering your experiences; the false beliefs you're holding onto, accompanied by painful memories and emotional traumas that give the old self continuity.

Emotional baggage is the residue of your fear-based perception. Wiping the illusions of the past from your windows of perception is essential for you to be able to experience the peace of God in the here and now.

Past pain comes into awareness to be transmuted in waves as you progress in your process. One step at a time is divine; no need to drop everything at the same time. Remember, the Great Pyramid was built one *stone* at a time, so too, is the kingdom of heaven realised within you progressively; *don't* rush yourself.

In the Bhagavad Gita, the divine in the form of Lord Krishna defines the spiritual path as the battle of right action. He teaches that along with worldly duties, one should perform activities that fan the flames of divine joy within them. To do this effectively, you need to become aware of your motivations in life. If you're reading this, then it's time to be honest with yourself; why are you doing what you do? What is it that drives you?

To become wholly absorbed in the here and now, during activity, put your full concentration on its performance and allow the result to come of its own accord. Everything we need, on a soul level, finds its way to us in divine timing if we trust how our life is unfolding. Letting go, paradoxically, gives you everything you want, in your heart of hearts. Chasing things out of fear usually only creates more barriers between you and your destiny.

Many differentiate between surrender and creation, but they fail to realise that being *is* creating, as your core vibration brings *all else unto you*, as Jesus said, exactly when you need it. The higher self knows what you need because it *is* you!

The ego may *believe* it knows what its outer purpose is in this life, but more often than not, it perceives the present through the eyes of the past, thus colouring its perception of what is. If this is the case, then it cannot possibly know its purpose, because fear-based motives and impulses generate most of its desires. The old self convinces you to hold onto the impressions of the past due to its fear of the unknown. The soul, however, doesn't operate on fear. You're expressing your true nature when you live in a state of non-resistance to the ever-changing scenes of the cosmic drama.

What does all this have to do with God? Everything, because it's only when you're in a state of balance, are you capable of becoming a conduit for divine creativity and inspiration. In such a state, you naturally feel attracted to the performance of joy-producing activities with no selfish motives as opposed to actions motivated by anxiety that are plagued by them. The past doesn't dictate who you are in the present moment whatsoever when you realise your innate timelessness, and that's what our true selves are, and most importantly, what the source is, *beyond* time.

When one acts on their passion, like me writing this book, for example, if done in the correct state, the performance of the action is effortless; time feels non-existent. In the creative state, one is channelling the wisdom of the divine *through* the medium of their higher self. It's also in this state that all great works of art and literature are created. One realises that they're not the doer, but the witness, observing the divine work *through* them.

"I have no sense of pleasure or pain, and I stay as I have always been. Sometimes He draws me outside and sometimes He takes me inside and I am completely withdrawn. I am nobody, all my actions are done by Him and not me."

– Sri Anandamayi Ma

In this state, the divine is the doer of all actions; it's writing the book through me and reading it through you. The inspiration, wisdom and creative spark come directly from the higher self, which is the intelligence of the soul, a drop in the ocean of cosmic consciousness.

"That yogi stays eternally in Me, who anchored in divine union (perfectly balanced between the physical and the higher self) and whatever his mode of existence, he then perceives me pervading the hearts of all beings."
–Bhagavad Gita 6:31

God is the source of everything; it is formless yet all forms simultaneously. If someone feels a resonance toward a God-realised master such as Christ, Krishna, Mother Mary, Mahavatar Babaji, Yogananda or Buddha, for example, they should see where that takes them. Masters and symbols of God resonate with a person for a reason. We never resonate with anything merely by chance or accident as coincidences don't exist. Masters of this magnitude became vessels for wisdom as they dissolved their time bound conditioning and became *yoked* with their higher selves; this is *yoga* (union with the divine).

Consciousness is a new word for the divine. Many today don't like to use the word God as there are countless limiting definitions attached to it. If you don't like the word, then use something else. Labels themselves mean nothing; however, if you haven't experienced the divine within yourself, then you'll never know the reality they are describing.

"Holiness consists simply in doing God's will and being just what God wants us to be."
— *St Thérèse de Lisieux*

The only way you can relate to the divine incorrectly is by attempting to connect to it in a way that doesn't work for you. But even that kind of experience can be helpful if you use it as contrast to show you how you can relate to it in a way that *does*. It's important to follow your heart and preferences, regardless of what those around you believe or say.

So, if you feel attracted to a form of God, see where it takes you. If the attraction comes from a place of joy, then it will work wonders for you. Others prefer to relate to God or the Goddess as Mother Nature or a supreme white light that pervades everything. All forms are ultimately symbols of your own highest potential. Imagine the highest ideal of yourself; that is God, who became you, *being* you. Use the symbols as reminders to live in the present and align with the best version of yourself as often as you can.

You have eternity to become aware of your oneness with the source; why be in a rush? I say this because one discovers the divine within themselves when they're ready. Yes, if one is truly passionate about the source, they should endeavour to connect to it every day, but they must also *trust* in the timing they reach each level of perception. This process can't be rushed; go easy on yourself.

One should never impose their religious or spiritual beliefs on others as many aren't ready but also remember that not all who wander are lost. You'll most likely put them off the idea altogether if you attempt to shove your beliefs down their throat. Live your truth and allow your *example* to pull those souls who need your support to find you exactly when they need you.

"God has no religion."
— *Mahatma Gandhi*

There's also no need to be religious out of fear, most are because they fear what might happen to them after they die; they're afraid of going to hell and burning for eternity. What they fail to realise, however, that hell is the very fear they're embodying. Think about this, if we reap what we sow, then how can a finite cause have an infinite effect? It is simply *not* possible. The concept of eternal damnation is just a fear-based belief; did it originate from someone's experience, or did it come from a misinterpretation of scripture? The blind cannot lead the blind, and when it comes to the divine, most are indeed *still* blind, unfortunately. People regain their sight by sipping on the divine elixir in the core of their being. When they nourish the godly seed in their heart with love and compassion for all, they realise that the source is love.

GROUNDING

Grounding is an idea often mentioned in new age communities, and people generally have a basic understanding of what it means to be grounded. What I'd like to expand upon here, however, is *why* it's essential to stay grounded, to be down to earth and level-headed on the spiritual path. Fanaticism and seriousness only take a person further from themselves.

To be grounded means to be *balanced*, to be aware that changes can occur in your life at any moment, as change is the only constant in creation. When your joy, bliss, love, creativity, and inspiration springs from the tranquil waters of peace, then it is genuine. Anxiety often motivates an individual's actions. To create out of stress, however, takes you further from who you really are. When you create out of fear, you're anchored in contrast rather than your light. The extent to which you can let go and be at peace determines the degree of faith you have in your process. Acting from peace and harmony with life pulls you towards joy-producing actions, because to be at peace is to embody your authentic self. When motivated by fear, you unconsciously act via *impulse*.

So, it's essential to stay grounded and remain level-headed. Being grounded is also synonymous to living in the present moment while expressing your childlike nature. The easiest way to anchor your awareness in the present is to do what you love. We all have worldly duties such as washing the dishes, taking the kids to school, walking the dog, and so on. Actions such as these, however, can be *redefined* and looked at as valid aspects of your joy. Taking care of your home, your kids, and your pets, for example, are essential for your happiness whether you're aware of it or not. The soul is unconditional love; it loves to nurture others. Krishna, in the Gita, spoke of this when he said to his disciple, Arjuna:

"The state of actionlessness isn't achieved by avoiding action. By forsaking work, nobody ever realises the state of perfection."
– Bhagavad Gita 3:4

Identification with the old self makes the ordinary tasks of life seem mundane; redefine them as essential aspects of your life. Including these duties, there will also be creative endeavours you'll feel the urge to do. Listen to these nudges from the higher self; they are your *calling*! You'll find that while you're in the performance of these actions that your consciousness is thrust effortlessly into the present moment. The more you're able to get into this creative state, the quicker you'll burn away the residue of your past.

"Before Enlightenment chop wood, carry water, after Enlightenment, chop wood, carry water."
– Zen Proverb

There are many methods people use to ground themselves, and they are all valid. Some will work for you and others won't. Stick with whatever works best for you. There's no one way to ground oneself; some prefer to work with crystals; others like to walk barefoot on the earth or meditate and visualise their root chakra connecting to the earth's core. I love running, meditation and writing; they help ground me as they are aspects of my passion. By embodying the creative state as much as I can, it's transformed my life more than anything else. It all depends on what you *believe* will work best for you. If you don't believe in the power of crystals, for example, then they won't do anything for you. It's essential to use only the tools and techniques that align with your belief system.

What does this word *grounding* mean? Does it imply to be brought down to earth? Not really, because if one is too grounded then they can't move; it's all about finding a *balance*. We have *two* minds; a physical mind which is synonymous with the ego and a nonphysical mind; the higher self. To be grounded is to be balanced between the mind that focuses you in the present with the higher self, guiding it from a nonlinear standpoint. To be grounded is to have your awareness centred between heaven and the earth; when you bring them together, you're expressing your true self.

We must learn to accept what's before us and then act *from* that state of acceptance. Whatever is in front of us is the result of our karma; how we've created our life thus far. Our perception of the outer world reflects our state of consciousness. To change what's in front of us, we must first *accept* what is. Being grounded is the best way to make changes in life because it's only in this state that infinite possibilities are open for us. Reality becomes more malleable when we don't take it so seriously, hence why I mentioned expressing our childlike nature earlier. To *play* with life is the key to making the changes you prefer more easily. Life is a gift bestowed upon us by the divine, don't struggle or endure it, *enjoy* it!

When we're imbalanced, we're usually at the whims of limiting beliefs in the unconscious. So, whenever you notice that you're not grounded as some may say, check your feelings, and root out the unconscious perceptions that have thrown you off balance. One of the best ways to ground yourself is to; first, *identify* the definitions creating the imbalance. Once you bring them into awareness, you'll most likely see how ridiculous it is to believe such things. When you realise the fallacy of the beliefs, embody your natural state of joy and appreciation. Open your heart and *allow* the divine to intoxicate you with its bliss.

Mother Nature is divine; we all feel at *home* in her embrace. I suggest that people be around nature as much as they can. Whether at the beach, the woods, or climbing mountains, even just a park with a few trees; she can bring you back into balance. Being around nature grounds us, and it's no coincidence that people who live in concrete jungles find themselves far more stressed out than those who lived in secluded areas. It's because they're not grounded anywhere near as much as the indigenous people. The state of balance is fundamental for being at peace and discovering true freedom.

GUILT AND SHAME

Guilt is an emotion we've all felt at some point in our lives, as none of us are without error; we all make mistakes. Sometimes, these mistakes can be at the expense of others, and especially those closest to us. Keeping the emotion bottled up, however, locks us in a devastating cycle of guilt and shame, which creates a tremendous amount of suffering. The guilty state degenerates our immune system, depleting our health in the process. Stress hormones weaken our white blood cells as they consume most of our energy to give the brain and body a rush of their chemical cocktails, over time, we become addicted to them.

Guilt is created by our perception of the world the moment it arises within us. So, if you're feeling guilty, it means that you believe you've done something wrong. Maybe you've made a mistake, try not to beat yourself up, as most experiences have the potential to be learning curves. They are opportunities to better ourselves if we're willing to learn from them. Learning from mistakes is essential, because if we don't, then we're going to have to repeat them.

"As a dog returneth to his vomit, so a fool returneth to his folly."

– Proverbs 26:11

Many repeat the same mistakes until they've suffered enough to generate the desire to make the changes required. All this suffering isn't necessary; however. We're perfectly capable of learning from a mistake the first time we make it; we shouldn't have to repeat them. We must become more conscious of the choices we make in life by questioning our perception, as it's the foundation of our behaviour. The development of any person depends on their ability to learn from their experiences.

Repeating mistakes slows growth down, learning quickly accelerates the process. You can even learn from other people's mistakes, this is how you use the bad examples of others in a positive way, by not falling down the same trapdoors they did!

Most of the guilt we feel is an *illusion*. We only create it because we believe, on some level that we must suffer to be who we truly are. Sometimes, we feel shame for the frailties that are part and parcel of the human condition. Some of us are even manipulated by others to feel guilty for being true to ourselves. Such is the state of our society today. Many who lack the courage to be their authentic selves play mind games with those who do.

> *"And a man's foes shall be they of his own household."*
> *– Matthew 10:36*

This dynamic is one of the challenges a person faces as they begin to awaken. Most of the people around them will, in some way, shape or form, attempt to *convince* them to feel guilty for standing out from the crowd. Many are afraid to take the leap of being who they really are for this reason; they fear being ostracised by those around them. Let me assure you, though, that if anyone abandons you for being true to yourself, it's a blessing to have them out of your life. Those who truly matter won't care, those who care *don't* matter.

If you feel guilty, then it's vital to become aware of the beliefs generating it. Are they your ideas creating the guilt or someone else's? If you discover that the guilt is your own, then work *with* it. Dissociating from emotions never works, as nothing ever goes away until it's taught you what it needs to.

Let me just add that I don't expect anyone reading this book to investigate *every* emotion they feel, that would be exhausting. I encourage you to go at whatever rate you feel comfortable. Don't rush yourself. When you feel it's time to open the can of worms, then do so. Sometimes, distracting yourself can be vital for your sanity. Play video games or sports, go running or watch TV; do something to take your mind off things if you don't feel ready to integrate the old self.

So, when you feel ready, work with the guilt to discover what it's trying to teach you. Make your guilt a valid aspect of the human condition. Every fear-based emotion in the body is there to show you something important about yourself; otherwise, it wouldn't be there, but I repeat, go at the rate you *feel* comfortable.

Every action has *consequences*; positive or negative. We must consider how our choices are going to influence those around us before making them. If we make correct choices, then we won't feel guilty as the emotion only arises when we're either buying into something that isn't our own or have behaved in ways we know we shouldn't have. If you're aligned with your integrity, then it doesn't matter what others think or say. Stand up for what you believe is true, but just make sure the ideals you're standing up for are your own!

People often keep negative energy bottled up inside them by attempting to remain oblivious to it. They refuse to work with this emotional residue, and as a result, become trapped in a vicious cycle of guilt and shame. They feel the guilt as *regret* and beat themselves up by feeling shame for their misconduct. Don't get me wrong, it's normal for any person to feel these emotions, but refusing to work with them only creates a deeper hole. The longer people hold onto negative emotional patterns; the more reinforced they become in the subconscious.

Redefining memories that trigger these emotions in the body is key. People need to change the way they look at their memories, by seeing them for what they taught them instead of loathing over them. When a person understands and learns the lessons in their painful experiences, they have an easier time *validating* them. They'll no longer *resent* or resist the experiences because they see that the challenging times have contributed to making them more aware of themselves; thus, have served a positive purpose.

Every experience has the potential to teach us something if we're willing to tweak our perspective and see it in the right light; our definitions determine what we get out of them. Learning the art of redefining situations, so they prove beneficial to our development is the key to playing with the building blocks of creation in the toy chest of our unconscious. We're here to *play* with physical reality by creating our life consciously.

The main motive behind me writing this book is to encourage people to accept the emotions that arise in their body. Doing this gives them a much easier time identifying the fears and beliefs at their source. Once they muster up the courage to embrace their feelings to discover those templates that have been hijacking their perception, perhaps for years, they'll laugh when they see just how absurd they are.

Many give themselves a hard time for not measuring up to the standards of perfection drilled into their minds by others. Let me tell you, however, that perfection is *subjective*. There is only one way to be perfect, and that's to be yourself. If this is true, that means perfection for every one of us is different. Who cares if you don't measure up to another's standards? Many of the lofty standards people set for themselves as a result of blindly believing in other's views are far too high. They desire to jump from A-Z right away; thus, attempt to live up to the standards and ideals of Z while they're on B; they then feel shame for not being able to measure up to those standards.

Trust in divine timing is the innate understanding that we're always exactly where we need to be. It's also true that everything happens in our life when it needs to happen and not a second before. Fears and beliefs, you've suppressed for years, for example, come into the light of your awareness when you're ready to integrate them. Your process is laid out for you, meticulously by the higher self. All you have to do is trust in the timing that everything happens. There are no coincidences in life; the steppingstones are gracefully laid down by the divine for you to stand on exactly when you need to. So, you're where you need to be right now; your imperfections are *perfect*. Own them, as overcoming these imperfections moulds you as a person. In the words of Christ; be of good cheer! You're *allowed* to be a masterpiece and a work in progress at the same time.

> **"God does not play dice with the universe."**
> *– Albert Einstein*

When you learn what the guilt is attempting to teach you, embody appreciation to life for teaching you another valuable lesson. The earth is a school, and her tests can be tough, but when we pass them, it's worth *every* bit of difficulty we went through. Learn to work with whatever existence lays before you, as it isn't thrown at you by random. Your life is planned out by forces your thinking mind isn't capable of comprehending. Only when you flow with the river of life, do you discover who you are.

HABITS

Most find changing habits *beyond* challenging; why is this? There are a few reasons; first, their belief that patterns are hard to change creates more difficulty than there needs to be. By defining the process in such a way, they defeat themselves before they even begin. Secondly, their approach never deals with the core of their issues; one must get beneath the pattern to see the unconscious processes convincing them to perpetuate it. Forcing oneself to change by suppressing impulses not only doesn't work but makes the process more difficult when one relapses. The self-defeatism reinforces the habit in the subconscious even stronger. Krishna, in the Bhagavad Gita, was referring to this suppression when he said to his chief disciple, Arjuna:

"The man who controls his organs of action by brute force, whose mind is always thinking thoughts of the sense objects he's attempting to stay clear of, is nothing but a hypocrite deluding himself."
– Bhagavad Gita 3:6

All habits have beliefs reinforcing them, as your behaviour reflects your state of consciousness. The most fundamental level of these processes are the beliefs in the unconscious. Altering the configuration of the ideas that don't serve you, enables you to behave in the ways you prefer to more easily. This process is the foundation of CBT (Cognitive Behaviour Therapy) in modern psychology. When you're in the process of changing a deeply ingrained habit, the beliefs generating it will try to convince you to remain *motivated* to perpetuate it, even though it's not what you prefer.

Becoming conscious of *why* you keep perpetuating the patterns you don't prefer is vital to unlocking yourself from their stranglehold on your consciousness. I'm not only going to show you why habits are much easier to change than people believe but also *how* to do it.

Let's say, for example, you have eating habits that you know will put your health in jeopardy if you perpetuate them. You grew up in a home where your mother always filled the cupboards with junk food. Every time you visit her house, resembling a robot, you move into the kitchen to grab cookies, crisps, and chocolate. You *seem* to have no control over yourself. Why would you keep choosing to eat in such a way, when you *know* it's not benefiting you? Maybe you don't believe that eating in such ways is dangerous, because everyone else in the house does it? Perhaps you don't think you *are* what you eat? Is there a lack of self-love convincing you to harm yourself by eating poorly? Maybe you're comfort eating to cover up some form of anxiety?

There could be a host of reasons why you're motivated to eat the junk in those cupboards. You'll only be capable of bringing those reasons into awareness when you're honest with yourself. Making the unconscious processes generating the habit, *conscious*, is the first step you must take in changing these patterns.

Once your motivations change, your behaviour will follow; being motivated correctly is essential to alter the habits you don't prefer to hold onto anymore. It would help if you got in touch with *why* you believe the opposite of change is more desirable when you know it isn't. There is always an underlying motivation fuelling patterns, even if you don't see them, they are there, pulling strings behind the curtains of your unconscious.

How are self-sabotaging habits formed? They are the result of your motives distorted by misaligned perceptions. Repetition of those actions crystallises them into the subconscious mind to enable you to do them without much effort. Habits are neutral; they aren't all negative. The power of the subconscious is extraordinary when you know how to programme it. The ability to walk or breathe without needing to think, for example, are automatic programmes in the subconscious.

Man is a creature, primarily of *habit*. Nothing controls our lives more than the patterns we consciously, or unconsciously choose to perpetuate: the subconscious and unconscious mind control around 95% of our behaviour, with the conscious mind, only having 5% of our energy to work with each day. Through self-observation, recognising one's redundant patterns and replacing them with healthier, productive, goal-oriented habits is pivotal to realising your purpose in life. Dreams without hard work, dedication and healthy habits *remain* just dreams.

Many of our habits are unconscious, which means we don't see them. When you become aware of a pattern, however, then it becomes a *choice*. If you have an addiction and recognise it, yet continue to perpetuate it, then it means that on some level, you're choosing it. You must get in touch with *why* you believe prolonging the behaviour is better than the alternative.

Beliefs form the motives behind these habits because you *always* feel motivated to act in ways that you believe serves you best, at any given moment. So, to change your motivations, you must become aware of the beliefs generating them. Beliefs and definitions are templates; they overlap our perception as we filter the external stimuli, we perceive with the senses *through* them. Our perception reflects our state of being, what we're believing at any moment.

This book is repetitive like I mentioned in the introduction, and that's because I want this information to become *habitual* to you. The more this knowledge is in your brain, the better chance you'll have of applying it to your life. Let's free ourselves of the habits that keep us attached to a life we don't prefer and rebuild our inner world with positive, healthier habits and perceptions.

When you were a child, your parents probably taught you the importance of brushing your teeth. For a few months, they would remind you every morning and evening to clean them. Eventually, the act becomes *routine*; this is all it takes to reprogram the subconscious mind. Replace your bad habits with healthier ones.

In 2010, I quit taking drugs and drinking alcohol, I started jogging three times a week and it was tough. My lungs felt like they were on fire the first time I ran, but I *persevered*. As the weeks and months went by, I grew fitter. By the time 2011 came, I could run 10 miles, (16km) without stopping! You can't go back to eating the stale cheese once you've tasted the good cheese. When you realise that your bad habits are like stale cheese which snatch away your peace and healthier habits raise your vibration, you'll have more of a desire to perpetuate ones that benefit you.

I encourage you to be light-hearted; treat this process as a game. Reprogramming yourself can be fun if seen in the right light; your human self is your *avatar* in this cosmic game. Customise him or her in the way you prefer to. Many in spiritual communities focus solely on embodying soul consciousness, but to me, this approach is *imbalanced*. You'll always be a consciousness, but you won't always be a person. Dive into pure consciousness from time to time to draw information from your higher self, for sure, but also play your part as a human being in all its variations. The ego is *divine;* you shouldn't need to kill your individuality to be at peace. We *can* have a foot in each realm; be human and divine, at the same time.

Now, I'm going to share with you an ancient technique that may be of some use to you. This method, combined with everything else I've mentioned in this chapter, will surely *untangle* you from any habit you have the desire to dissolve; your willingness is an essential part of the process.

As you lay in bed at night, before sleeping, lay flat on your back, and close your eyes. Now, can you imagine how you would feel if you were *already* free of the habit? How would you *feel* if you were the version of yourself you desire to be? What is their state of being? Can you attune to it? Remember, that linear time is an illusion; all versions of you already exist. Embody the state; *feel* what it would be like to be the person you prefer; think the thoughts you'd be thinking if you were that version. Imagine a friend, visualise them before you; converse with them in your imagination, *hear* their voice. Tell them that you used to have the habit and that you've overcome it, and that you'll never go back to it again. Imagine them congratulating you; shake their hand, hug them, smell their hair as they embrace you. Visualise what would *happen* in the outer world if you were that version of yourself.

Fall asleep in the feeling of freedom and do it every night until you are. If you desire to be free of illegal substances, alcohol, pornography, or anything else you feel isn't aligned with your integrity, fall asleep *as* that version of yourself. When you're in bed in that lucid state between sleep and waking where you get *beyond* yourself, you're in the domain of the Quantum Field. If you persist in falling asleep in the assumption of freedom, it eventually rewires the subconscious; thus, your beliefs and motivations *automatically* change. You can use this technique to achieve anything you desire; I've placed it in the habit section because I feel it's a great way of letting go of those habits that bind us to versions of ourselves, we don't prefer.

HEAVEN AND HELL

The concept of heaven is greatly misunderstood, with its opposite, hell even *more* so. Most religious people around the globe misinterpret their scriptures when they speak of heaven and hell. Now, I'm not implying that there aren't any heavenly or hellish realms in existence, there might be. The context in which the scriptures and the masters teach them, however, are states of being, *not* locations.

> *"Neither shall they say, Lo here! Or, lo there! For, behold, the kingdom of God is within you."*
> *– Luke 17:21*

To be in hell is to live with fear-based beliefs hijacking your perception. Most resist their authentic self because they don't have the courage to express it, or they lack the awareness to know what it is. Many living today are actually *in* hell, as their conditioning controls their perception of the environment, compromising their lives in the process. Being tossed and turned by the tumultuous waves of life, the only peace they experience is dependent on outer circumstances; when this happens, the external world controls their state of being. Any joy or peace they manage to obtain is eventually snatched away by the inevitable situations that manifest to highlight their misalignment. If they were to realise that it's merely the way they *define* the ups and downs that create the emotional storms, they'd be *willing* to change their perception of them.

If only people would cease allowing outer circumstances to determine their state of being, then they'd know true peace, as their joy wouldn't be dependent on what happens to them. They'd go beyond the need for triggers, which is the key to discovering the kingdom of heaven in physical reality. Most people's focus is primarily on the surface of their body via their senses, and not within it. Many who claim to be spiritual, still believe their body is all they are. They define themselves, and their whole being via their mind's processes and their body, as they're entirely oblivious to their oneness with the higher self; to live in such a state is *hell*. Resisting the guidance of the nonlinear self does nothing but create brick walls for you to smash into; thus, you suffer. This is the most exhausting thing you can do, and especially if you've adopted a victim mentality. Resentment, anger, hatred, and victimisation are side-effects of a lack of awareness of your innate oneness with the source.

> ***"Resistance is Hell, for it places man in a 'state of torment'."***
> *– Florence Scovel Shinn*

This experience doesn't have to be defined negatively, however. Why do we create the experience of misalignment? To give us *contrast*; we have a better time discerning what's true for us when we've experienced what's not, *first*. We must experience the fires of hell to enable us to perceive the gates of heaven. The amount of contrast you need to see what's right for you is up to you. You can learn your lessons now if you want to. Many prefer to hit rock bottom before making the required changes, but it isn't necessary.

> ***"The Kingdom of Heaven is within you, and whosoever shall know himself shall find it."***
> *– Ancient Egyptian Proverb*

Only when you're living from your centre are you capable of enjoying life. To be centred is to be *balanced* between the mind and the higher self; thus, the soul is free to express itself. When you find that balance and enjoy the effortlessness that comes along with it, you're in your essence. In this state, you know, deep within the core of your being, that you're an eternal child of the infinite spirit. You dive into the silence at times to draw wisdom, guidance and inspiration from the inner self and come back out into the world with a smile in your heart.

When you live in this state, you also become the conscious creator of your life, which means you're no longer a victim to your own power. People victimise themselves when they're unconsciously creating their reality by accidently manifesting unfavourable circumstances and playing the blame game on God or other people. They must learn how to *tame* their imagination; because until they do, they'll continue creating more contrast for themselves.

Let's say, for example, you manifest a hefty load of cash, all of a sudden you feel worthy, happy and blessed. Six months later, something happens that forces you to go bankrupt so that you lose every penny; suddenly, you feel worthless again. The danger in allowing outer circumstances to determine our happiness is that all experiences, no matter how great or awful, are transitory, thus, *unreliable*.

"Lay not up for yourselves treasures upon earth, where moth and rust doth corrupt, and where thieves break through and steal: But lay up for yourselves treasures in heaven, where neither moth nor rust doth corrupt, and where thieves do not break through nor steal: For where your treasure is, there will your heart be also."
– *Matthew 6:19-21*

You're worthy regardless of what you possess. This example is just one of the many illusions the old self has programmed into it. When you can embody the peace of God regardless of what's happening, then you're breaking free of its stranglehold on your consciousness.

When you're present, acting on your joy without expectations, then you're flowing with life in a state of vulnerability. In the words of Yogananda, you attune to your very own *portable paradise*. The bliss in your heart is always there, waiting for you to sip upon its heavenly elixir; it never leaves you. You often overlook it as the ramblings of your old self *distract* you. Once you know how to activate this joy, you'll obtain the *keys* to the kingdom of God; this state of being is Yoga, Zen, your true self.

When people are misaligned, they chase sensory pleasures with the hope they'll give them the fulfilment they desire; this is an illusion, though, as all experiences in the world are *transitory*. Pleasures come and go just like everything else experienced through the senses. Sooner or later, they chase something else to try and satisfy their longing; the cycle goes on until they're on their deathbed regretting all the time they wasted. This kind of thinking constitutes *mundane* desire; it's the belief that we're not whole within ourselves, so we chase an abundance of experiences with the hope that we can finally become whole again.

Don't get me wrong; there's nothing inherently *wrong* with enjoying the pleasures of the world, as long as your happiness isn't dependent on them; this is what it means to seek the kingdom of God *first*. When you discover that wholeness, which never left you, then you're free to play with the world and its experiences in a state of nonattachment because your desires won't come from a place of lack, but from wholeness and integrity. Any wishes that come from a sense of scarcity are not your true desires because you don't lack anything; you just *believe* you do.

The crown of thorns on the head of Christ represents the old self, which makes you *bleed* for experiences which have their root in misaligned beliefs. These beliefs convince you to aimlessly chase joy outside of yourself, only to have the little amount of joy you *do* find snatched from you sooner rather than later. Crucify these desires! They don't belong to you!

Christ is your true self and is only accessible in the present moment; be that Christ and be ye therefore perfect, even as your Father, which in heaven, is *perfect*. Christians have taken this idea out of context; their religion is full of allegory. Much of what the Bible says has more of an inner significance than an external one.

Jesus said the kingdom of God is *within* you; what he meant is that the everlasting joy of the soul is within you and nowhere else. You're a wave of the sea, and you carry a portable paradise in your heart. Identify with that bliss and play with the world; because taking the game of life too seriously is one of the biggest ways the old self keeps you burning in the fires of misalignment.

IMAGINATION

Everyone uses their imagination, sometimes consciously and other times unconsciously to manifest the events they experience in their lives. The imagination is the buffer *between* the physical mind and the higher self; many misuse it; however, as their thoughts reflect their worries most of the time.

Worry is the result of a distorted imagination, and thanks to such distortion people manifest experiences they don't prefer. Their fear *can* serve a purpose, though, if one is willing to become *conscious* of the thoughts generating it.

Anxiety is the body's way of telling you that you're imbalanced; it exists to point your awareness in the direction of the beliefs hijacking your perception. It's essential to become aware of the templates that colour the guidance sent to you from the higher self.

"I know of a man who feared a certain disease. It was a very rare disease and difficult to get, but he pictured it continually and read about it until it manifested in his body, and he died, the victim of distorted imagination."

– Florence Scovel Shinn

The imagination is our creative faculty, and if used consciously with the right intentions, you can manifest any experience you want. When you desire something, you need to use your imagination to generate the *state of being* of your wish fulfilled. Everything you can imagine exists in the here and now, in some reality, because if it didn't, you wouldn't be *capable* of imagining it. Living as if your dreams are already a reality is fundamental to manifesting them.

"Your assumption, to be effective, cannot be a single isolated act, it must be a maintained attitude of the wish fulfilled."

– Neville Goddard

Feel like you're already the person you *desire* to be. Don't think about them; see the world *through* their eyes. You can use your imagination to heal yourself, for example, if you're unwell, imagine that you're healthy and feel as light as a feather while thinking the thoughts you'd be thinking if you were. Persist in embodying that state as much as you can, and eventually, you'll witness your mind, body and health radically improve to match your new state.

Another benefit of holding onto the state you prefer is that you're reprogramming the subconscious by doing so. Holding onto new feelings untangles the hardwiring and patterns that keep you chained to the illusion of the past. It's very simple; all you need to do is notice when you're misaligned and embody the state of your wish fulfilled.

"Daring to assume that all things are possible to imagine, put this one reality to the extreme test by assuming you are the person you would like to be. Your reasonable mind and outer senses may deny it; but I promise you: if you will persist, you will receive your assumption. Believe me, you are the same God who created and sustains the universe, but are keyed low; so you must be persistent if you would bring about a change."

– Neville Goddard

Making your preferred state a habit is a process. You'll likely oscillate between joy and fear until you've crystallised your bliss as your most dominant. Be patient; the oscillation is a valid part of the process. When you fall in vibration, it's not because you've taken a step backwards, it's because you're going back down to pick up a valuable piece of information you forgot to take with you into the higher states. So, having gone down in vibration, paradoxically, you're still moving *forward* because you've become more aware of yourself; this only applies if you're actually *willing* to work with the contrast you're presented with, however.

Of course, it's going to be challenging initially; stepping out the comfort zone of your habitual state can be uncomfortable, but the challenge doesn't need to be defined negatively. Challenges are *exciting*; they prod us into the realisation of whom, and what we are, so we can draw upon the timeless power residing within our soul.

Your mind can be your best friend or your worst enemy; it depends on *how* you use it. In Catholic churches, it is not uncommon to see depictions of the Virgin Mary standing on a serpent in many of the paintings and statues. The serpent is our creative power, and it must be *tamed*. We must train ourselves to be more disciplined on the mental level; otherwise, we can harm ourselves by creating experiences we don't want, which is what many in our society individually, and collectively are doing. The unconscious use of the imagination is the reason the world is in the state it is today. We must become masters of our inner world. Indeed, it's mastery of *the word* that leads us to emancipation.

"Imagination and faith are the secrets of creation."

– Neville Goddard

Almost *everything* we experience is the result of our imaginings; life itself is a daydream of the soul. All our challenges, fears, worries and anxieties are on some level, *imagined*. We're capable of creating situations which bring us joy, wisdom, happiness and love, but our minds more easily side with the negativity of the world, but why does it? A victim mentality is to live in denial of your creative power, and you were probably brought up around people who have such a mindset. When you notice your mind being negative, go back to neutral and realign with your vision; it's that simple.

"We are shaped by our thoughts; we become what we think. When the mind is pure, joy follows like a shadow that never leaves."

– Buddha

We're here to use our imagination to bring more divine inspiration into this reality. Leaving this world, and our civilisation more loving, colourful, joyful, and *better* than it was when we entered it, is the duty of every generation. We must lay the foundation for the future and come up with new ways of going about things; otherwise, we've failed as a generation.

So, use your imagination wisely, the old saying *'be careful what you wish for'* comes to mind. Become more conscious of your self-talk and when you see that it's on the negative tracks *redirect* the train of your intention onto thoughts that are more joyful, productive and in agreement with your truth.

INTIMACY

Many define intimacy solely as being sexually active with another, but this is a shallow definition as far as I'm concerned. Real intimacy is to be vulnerable, and willing to embrace the unknown while holding the hand of another.

To be close with your partner is to *allow* them into your being. How do we accomplish this? Firstly, we must love and accept ourselves as we are. We also need to be at a place mentally, where no matter what happens in the relationship, we'll be *fine*. We need to go beyond defining ourselves through the eyes of others, and especially our partners because only when we do, are we capable of sharing divine love with them.

We're often incapable of knowing what's going to happen next in our lives, including our relationships. All relationships are insecure in this respect; life is uncertain by nature as we only experience it at its fullest when we smash through the glass ceiling of our comfort zone. We must transcend the familiar, however, if we're to realise our potential, which also means overcoming our greatest fears.

Most in our society today are fickle and indecisive when it comes to love and relationships; it's common for couples to break up after just a couple of months of being together. Maybe the people in the relationship aren't right for one another, which is fine, as with every experience of this kind, we move closer to realising our preference in another. Most of the time, we have a better time knowing what we prefer by experiencing what we don't first by contrast. In some cases, though, couples break up because they lack the courage to *face* the baggage that surfaces in the relationship.

Our most intimate relationships, (they don't have to be romantic) bring out the limiting beliefs in our unconscious that sabotage our experience of life. Limiting beliefs, fears, emotional patterns, and redundant habits, are brought into consciousness when we're around those we hold most dear, as we've all contributed to conditioning each other in the past. Tendencies spawned by limiting beliefs often reinforce themselves when they encounter themselves in others.

An empowered relationship is a union where both people understand that they could lose their partner at any moment. This inspires them to appreciate one another even more. In this universe of uncertainty, the ultimate test of death could tear them apart, or another person could come onto the scene. We're not capable of knowing what's around the corner in life; it's full of surprises. Those in an empowered relationship are also aware that whatever manifests in their life is needed for their evolution. If you're able to attract someone who's committed to improving themselves daily while simultaneously *accepting* who they are in the here and now, then you've hit the jackpot!

Honesty, acceptance, and the willingness to inspire one another for self-improvement sets the foundation for a truly intimate relationship. There must also be a strong mental connection; one that makes both partners feel like they're with themselves is pivotal to a long-lasting bond. If your minds aren't often on the same wavelength, then one or both of you aren't being vulnerable enough.

What causes people to fear vulnerability? Some in so-called intimate relationships feel ten brick walls between themselves and their partner. People put these walls up because they define themselves *through* the scope of their fear-based beliefs, thus, resembling a turtle, retreat into the shell of their comfort zone. If you're afraid of the person you supposedly love the most, however, then what's the point in being with them? You need to be more honest with yourself and *allow* your partner to see your frailties as we all have them; they are part and parcel of the human condition. People who judge you for your shadow are only condemning the same darkness within themselves. No one is perfect, yet that imperfection *is* perfection, as it forces us to be dependent on our connection to the source.

In a successful union, both partners work as a team; they don't become subconscious enemies. Physical reality reflects the processes in our unconscious through the synchronicity, circumstances, and our closest relationships. Both in a relationship must take responsibility for the skeletons in the closet of their unconscious and cease playing the blame game. In facing their darkness head-on together, inspiring, uplifting and forgiving one another when needed, progress is *guaranteed.*

Intimacy is ultimately the willingness to be your true self regardless of who's in front of you. Everyone in your reality is an aspect of your consciousness. When people are afraid to be intimate, it's because they're scared to express their true selves. Many have an unconscious fear that if they become who the source intends them to be and not another cog in the engine of society, they'll be shunned by those around them. Ironically, by doing this, however, they're isolating themselves from the collective consciousness.

Be who you are regardless of who's around you; those who matter and are relevant to your life, will stay, love and accept you as you are. Even Christ had haters; they reviled him so much that they nailed him to a cross; it can't be avoided, as we're incapable of pleasing everyone. So, shine anyway; transcend the hate, be a living example to those around you that it is, indeed, beautiful to be who you are.

KARMA

What is *karma*? How do most define this concept? Wherever I go, I see people adopting a fatalistic attitude with their perspective of karma. Most equate it with punishment, judgement, and divine retribution; it's my belief, however, that these definitions are outdated. They originate from a medieval age, plagued in superstitions, religious dogmas, and spiritual misunderstandings. If man is to take responsibility for what he's emitting out into the universe, then definitions like these must be dropped. Karma isn't a disciplinary system set up by some God sitting on his laptop, recording our transgressions in a confined corner of space-time; it's the law that our perception of the outer world reflects our state of consciousness. What you give, you shall receive, or to put it in Biblical terms; man reaps what he *sows*.

> *"Be not deceived; God is not mocked: for whatsoever a man soweth, that shall he also reap."*
> *– Galatians 6:7*

The word karma originates from the ancient language of *Sanskrit*—its definition is *action*. Every action we perform consciously or unconsciously originates in our mind. All activities are governed by our motivations, which in turn are formed by what we *believe* to be true. So, it's safe to say that our behaviour is a direct reflection of our perception, because we always behave in ways, we believe serves us best, at any given moment.

Behaviour is action in *motion*, made visible, tangible, or subject to form. Subtle and psychological forms of activity such as thinking, feeling, believing, and discerning form our perception. Beliefs are the blueprint level of our reality; they lay the foundation of the scope through which we filter the outer world.

Your state of being, at any given moment, emits a frequency into the universe. Many in *Law of Attraction* circles claim that our thoughts create our reality, but this is a shallow version of the truth as far as I'm concerned. One can think positively all they want, but if their feelings aren't in tandem with those thoughts, it will render them void. Emotion reflects one's conviction; their belief and if they aren't *feeling* their thoughts into being, then they don't believe what they're thinking.

The conscious mind is the level of conscious thoughts, the subconscious, which is the level above, governs our feelings, habits, and automatic thoughts. The universe is more likely to respond to our intentions when our thoughts and emotions are aligned. To achieve this alignment is to wed feminine and masculine together. When the subconscious and conscious minds are *yoked*, you discover Eden within. The woman or *womb* of creation, (the subconscious) serves her husband (conscious mind) into manifesting anything he believes he's capable of having.

Intention is everything; for example, if you were to walk down the road and step on ants without realising that you have, there'd be no karmic consequence as your intention was pure, nonetheless. But, if you deliberately stomp them all day, you'll not be punished by those actions in the way people think. The act will be stored and reinforced in your brain as an experience, though, and will manifest in different ways. The hatred which drove you to harm innocent creatures will reinforce itself in you. The more you strengthen any tendency, then the more difficult it is to overcome. Every experience we have affects our brain; one fear-based action has the potential to turn into many more. Karma works more on a psychological level than anything.

Addiction is another example of how this works. Imagine a man who was peer pressured into taking an illegal substance by his friends and gets loaded for the first time. Fast-forward five years later, and his life is in bits. He has no money, no job, no relationships and is still doing all he can to get his next fix. Whether he was peer pressured or not makes no difference, as it was his choice to do it. He decided to take the drug, and now, every time he does it, he makes that decision again. Why? It's because of how he's defining himself *in relation* to the substance.

Again, we come back to belief systems; maybe he believes he can't live without it? Perhaps a lack of self-love convinces him that he needs to suffer, so he punishes himself? He probably thinks he needs to numb himself from the onslaught of the outer world, as he defines himself as a victim to circumstances. As an ex-addict, I can testify that addictions and habits can be overcome if the person is willing to take an honest look at themselves, question their motives, along with having the *will* to change and the courage to embrace the unknown.

Another aspect of karma are the themes we've chosen to explore before incarnating. Our karmic blueprint contains all the lessons and experiences we wish to have as a physical being; but we're also capable of changing our blueprint by shifting to different timelines.

Karma is also related to *synchronicity*. If you have limiting beliefs attached to your perception, then the synchronicities in your life will reflect the misalignment. Life reflects our unconscious back unto us, and at times, brings us challenging circumstances to show us. This is why it's essential to keep a positive attitude towards all things that manifest as everything *can* serve us if seen in the right light. When we live in the present, all that is unconscious in us surfaces to be released.

Sometimes, you'll attract circumstances or see signs that reveal the limiting beliefs hiding in you. Karma, in this context, can be said to be a wake-up call; you must listen to their messages because the keys to unlocking yourself from the illusion of the past are in them.

So, cease defining karma as punishment. Let's work *with* the synchronicities that appear in our lives and perform conscious actions that enable us to overcome our challenges. Let's take responsibility for our state of being and drop the victim mentality because most of what we experience in life is the result of our own doing. Radiate loving intentions and the universe has no choice to reflect them unto you. Karma will then be a blessing to you as this will enable you to enjoy what you *reap* from your sowing.

KNOWLEDGE AND WISDOM

Knowledge and wisdom, are they different? Yes, in truth, they are poles apart. Firstly, knowledge is the information one learns from books, classes, and teachers. Wisdom, on the other hand, can't be learned, but only be realised through experience. The information in this book, for example, is *knowledge*. Discovering the truth contained within this work has nothing to do with just reading it, because until one applies it to their life; they won't truly know what I'm saying. Wisdom is acquired when one embodies their unique expression of the truth. It doesn't matter what I or anyone else says to another, if they aren't applying the knowledge to their life then they're wasting their time.

"And why call ye me, Lord, Lord, and do not the things which I say?"
– Luke 6:46

Many define intelligence based solely on how much a person can memorise, but to me, this isn't *real* intelligence. I define intelligence as the ability to observe yourself, act spontaneously, live life in the present moment and to apply the information you've learned intellectually to your life. It doesn't matter how many religious texts or self-help books you've read, nor does it matter how many lectures you listen to online. If you aren't applying the knowledge to your life, then it's all in vain.

"The highest form of human intelligence is to observe yourself without judgement."
– Jiddu Krishnamurti

How many teachers, life coaches, pastors, and priests, who have a large following are good at telling others how to live their lives but refuse to live the truth themselves? Hypocrisy seems to be a common theme today and especially religious people who condemn others for mistakes them, themselves, make daily. Christ himself pointed this out when he said:

"And why beholdest thou the mote that is in thy brother's eye, but considerest not the beam that is in thine own eye? Or how wilt thou say to thy brother, Let me pull out the mote out of thine eye; and, behold, a beam is in thine own eye? Thou hypocrite first cast out the beam out of thine own eye; and then shalt thou see clearly to cast out the mote out of thy brother's eye."

– Matthew 7:3-5

Emotional intelligence is true intelligence; when one can discern what their feelings are telling them without bias or distortion, they're in harmony with their inner self. Working with the emotions that arise in the body and finding the beliefs generating them is an experience that creates *wisdom*. Through this process, one can align with the version of themselves they prefer. We must make the unconscious, *conscious* by alchemising the emotional residue in us to align ourselves with our very own portable paradise. All wisdom exists *within* us. Only when we revert our focus from the outer world to our inner world are we capable of sipping from the divine spring in our hearts.

"Man know thyself; then thou shalt know the universe and God."

– Pythagoras

The educational systems today only teach children how to fit into the current economic system, which is on the verge of collapsing. Apart from the basics such as English, mathematics and a general understanding of science, we mostly learn things that we don't need. Kids usually know what their passion is from a tender age, I know I did, anyway. They should be encouraged to do what they love and taught how to observe themselves. Some schools are now introducing meditation and mindfulness to their curriculum, which is a positive start. Teaching people how to make money without also showing them how mastering their energy creates a stressful life; is it any wonder why addiction in all forms is soaring? You've learned how to be functional in the outer world while being *dysfunctional* in your inner world.

An essential aspect of the art of living is accepting the fear that arises in the body, to observe it *without* resistance. When one embraces the unknown, they become aware of how the laws of the universe operate when one allows them to. Life becomes effortless when you enjoy the rollercoaster of physical reality without fearing what might be coming next. Be so engrossed in the present moment that you don't even care!

> ***"To know thyself is the beginning of wisdom."***
> *– Socrates*

Love is the ultimate form of wisdom. Only through love and acceptance can one embrace the gift of life granted to them by the divine. Wisdom is nothing but *healed* pain, which adds fuel to the inferno of love that perpetually burns in the depths of their soul.

Humility is also a vital aspect of wisdom. To be humble is to understand that there's always more to learn. When a man loses his humility, and his pride takes him over, then his mind is closed off; he's no longer receptive to what life is trying to show him. One must empty their cup so the divine can fill it with its intelligence. Masters are content with knowing that they always know what they need to know, exactly *when* they need to know it. The key to understanding is the willingness to let go and know *nothing*.

"And whosoever shall exalt himself shall be abased; and he that humble himself shall be exalted."

– Matthew 23:12

Watch out when you begin to see yourself as wise; this is the alarm bell. Nobody can know everything; there's always someone who comes along who knows something you don't. Life is continuously humbling the man anchored in wisdom, as he's receptive and open to change when necessary. Humble yourself, or life *will* humble you.

LONELINESS

Many do all they can to avoid being alone, but they fail to realise that we're all alone, as there's ultimately only one being in existence. The illusion of separation is a valid one, but on the most fundamental level of reality, we're drops of the same ocean. Unique, yet one, we're all waves that emerge from the same sea of consciousness, the fabric of creation.

In a sense, each of us are in a subjective universe, as we all observe reality *through* our unique windows of perception. For example, two people can observe the same person, but each of them would see them in ways unique to themselves. As a result, they'd be observing different *versions* of that person filtered through their beliefs. Maybe one of them would see the best in the person they're observing, and perhaps the other would judge them for their human frailties; this happens because we usually don't see others as we are, but as *we* are. It's common for people to *project* their most dominant state onto those around them. The person who saw the best in the individual they observed, did so because they see it in themselves—with the other seeing the things they've yet to accept about themselves reflected at them.

In the dream state, everyone in it is a projection of your consciousness; so too is everyone in physical reality, the *daydream* of your soul. I wrote this book to help you bring your limiting beliefs into awareness, but you must also be wary of projecting them onto others. Because, in the deeper sense, there *are* no others, as what you believe about other people has the potential to manifest in your reality. If we're optimistic and send them good vibes, then good things *can* come to pass for them. This is what it means to *pray* for others; to believe in them.

"Therefore, all things whatsoever ye would that men should do to you, do ye even so to them: for this is the law and the prophets."
— *Matthew 7:12*

We're all directors and stars in this cosmic movie, and the other people, who are the co-stars in our life, often bend to our state of being. Christian mystic, *Neville Goddard*, understood this principle; that we create different *versions* of others in our reality as we change ourselves. We move to other versions of the earth the moment we alter ourselves, and on those different worlds are different versions of the people we know and love. Neville would close his eyes and *visualise* specific people stood before him in his imagination:

"I bring him before my mind's eye and I congratulate him on his good fortune because he is now gainfully employed. I allow him to accept my congratulations because I do not see a man unemployed, I see him employed and he knows he is in my mind's eye for in that state I have pruned him from the unemployed state and once more reshaped the branch that grows in the garden of God."
— *Neville Goddard*

This is where the *conscious* use of the imagination comes into play. How many people do you argue with between your ears? You can guarantee that imagining arguments will only manifest them in the outer world, sooner rather than later. We must *tame* the imagining faculty; as we may end up hurting ourselves and others with our negative thoughts, as they're projections of us. Be careful what you wish for; love thy neighbour as yourself because they *are* you.

"And thou shalt love the Lord thy God with all thy heart, and with all thy soul, and with all thy mind, and with all thy strength: this is the first commandment. And the second is like, namely this, Thou shalt love thy neighbour as thyself. There is none other commandment greater than these."
— *Mark 12:30-31*

Solitude is essential in life. Everyone should spend time alone, at least a couple times a week to recharge their energy levels. Interacting with others and working all week can drain us. It's wise to retreat within, into the silence, as it's there, in the void, that we discover who we are.

"Without great solitude, no serious work is possible."
– Pablo Picasso

How many are in relationships because they fear being alone? I know many who are in love not together, and many that aren't, who are. Married couples, for example, use the excuse that they're staying together for the kids, but it doesn't help anyone. If both partners are still miserable with each other after doing *all* they can to rebuild their relationship, they won't be capable of parenting their children to the best of their ability.

We're social creatures; of course, we're not supposed to be alone all the time. We're here to interact with the world, it's people and uplift society with our talents and the skill sets we develop. Healthy relationships are *essential* to fulfilling the needs of our human self. The kind of company you keep is vital to your development; surround yourself with those who inspire you to go *further*.

When you need to retreat, then do so. Learn to *love* solitude. People only fear it because their beliefs convince them that it's scary or unpleasant. It's essential to bring these beliefs into awareness. If you struggle to be alone, then start by being alone for an hour, then two hours and so on. You'll gradually begin to *appreciate* your solitude, and probably crave more of it. There's no better company than to be with yourself because when you're alone, you're in the presence of God, who dwells in the uttermost core of your being.

LOVE

Love is the finest quality we possess; in fact, it's what we truly are. Most, however, are oblivious to the love that resides within them, and as a result, fail to express their true nature. They don't know how to access the spring of divine love that perpetually gushes from the depths of their being. Love binds the entirety of creation together, uniting us as one family.

True love is complete freedom, and it starts with you. If you don't love and accept yourself as you are, then you're incapable of loving and accepting others as they are. So many are in resistance to their true selves, as they believe there's something *wrong* with them; the only thing wrong, however, is the fact that they've bought into this falsity.

Society convinces people to reject their true nature, but one doesn't have to answer to others. Seeking to fit in at the expense of your true self isn't fitting in at all but to ostracise yourself from the collective consciousness. You're in harmony with existence when you align with it, and through your example, you inspire others to do the same. To reject your true nature to fit in is quite simply the death of your God-given individuality. Thus, for one to express their true self, they're most likely going to have to be *rebellious* at times.

The divine created you as a masterpiece. On a higher level of consciousness, you, as the higher self, formed your physical self, including your appearance. All the imperfections you *believe* you have, the challenges you've faced in your life and the talents you possess, have been imprinted in your consciousness to design you as a masterpiece. Many are in resistance to themselves by refusing to express their innate divinity, as they'd rather fit into the collective unconscious than align with the collective consciousness.

"Before I formed thee in the belly I knew thee; and before thou camest forth out of the womb I sanctified thee, and I ordained thee a prophet unto the nations."
– Jeremiah 1:5

There are *no* coincidences in life. Even the experience of buying into limiting beliefs has the potential to be divine, as it gives you the contrast to recognise the version of yourself you prefer to align with. If there are certain aspects of yourself that you're in resistance to, then you need to work *with* this resistance. What's convincing you to shun your true self? What programmes have hijacked your perception? What psychological boundaries confine you to your comfort zone?

Many say they fear the dark, but if that were so, they'd be living their truth. People fear the light because they're addicted to being someone they're not. They fear being rejected by those around them but let me tell you that being shunned by those who refuse to accept you is a spiritual blessing in disguise.

Those we spend the most time with have a major influence on our personality. Everyone is copying and conditioning one another; limiting belief systems are being gobbled up left, right and centre. It's wise to keep your circle small, trustworthy and to be of service to anyone who sincerely asks for your support. If you desire to adopt a positive and enthusiastic mindset, then being around those who have a victim mentality all the time won't help you. Find those on the same path as you, instead of those who want to bring you down to their level; misery *loves* company.

Self-love is the beginning of freedom, because, when you love and accept yourself as you are, then you're beginning to move into agreement with your higher self. When you allow yourself to be who you truly are and not whom everyone else believes you *should* be, then you find your true self, hiding in the centre of the labyrinth formed by society's lies encircling your essence.

"You yourself, as much as anybody else in the entire universe, deserve your love and affection."
– Buddha

When it comes to other people, it's essential to realise that our most important relationship is the one we have with ourselves. The experience of being in a relationship where two people are with each other because they fear loneliness, for example, is a valid one, as it teaches us much by contrast. The only question is, how *many* of these is it going to take for you to start taking responsibility for your happiness?

When one reaches a decent level of self-acceptance, they become less dependent on others for their happiness. They rely solely on their connection to the source, and not the validation they believed they needed to fit in.

"Life is uncertain, and so are the situations, everything keeps changing. If you are aware, you can learn a lot from life: awareness makes you mature, patient and helps you grow and develop wisdom. Love is the most essential part of spirituality. Love everyone, love God."

– Guru Ma, Ritu

To live our life to the fullest, we must *accept* ourselves. Life truly begins when we embrace the unknown by mastering the art of living in the present moment. Mentally brooding on the past only keeps us away from who we truly are. The past is contrast; the present is the portal to the true self.

When you love and accept yourself, then you can do nothing but love everyone else. Projection works both ways, not just in the negative as some have suggested. Everyone in physical reality is a mirror of ourselves, if you genuinely love and accept yourself, then the people will reflect that self-love at you. Now, this doesn't mean everyone will be nice to you—but the way you *respond* to them will always be for the greater good; even if it means telling them to go away.

Only love can prevent our civilisation from destroying itself. We must put all our differences aside and accept one another as we are; including our imperfections, as they are valid aspects of the human condition. Many say religion divides our civilisation, and this may be true on some level. This is only so, however, because most of humanity believes that if one set of beliefs are correct, that if any others which contradict them must be incorrect. *Cognitive dissonance* is the real enemy of humanity if there is one, because it's fuelled all the religious wars and terrible onslaughts throughout our history.

"The truth is like a Lion, you don't have to defend it. Let it loose. It will defend itself."
– St Augustine

When one becomes aware of the true nature of physical reality, they gladly give everyone the space to believe what they want, as they realise that each of us live in a subjective reality. When they become aware of this, they align with their truth, and it becomes unshakable. If anybody can shake your truth, then it isn't yours, as your integrity is unchangeable. So why not express it? Love is the true *saviour,* as it's only when you love yourself do you go *beyond* the lies society has drilled into your mind.

MANIFESTING

Everyone is the creator of their lives, whether they're aware of it or not. All the experiences they manifest reflect either their karmic blueprint or what they're putting out into the universe via their state of being. For people to become conscious creators, they must take *responsibility* for their emotional state, which means they must drop the victim mentality prevalent in our society. To play the victim to the circumstances you, yourself bring into manifestation is to disempower yourself by being in denial of your creative power.

"Have you realised that you are the creator of your reality? And that you have the power to re-create it as well?"
– Ayako Sekino

If an undesirable circumstance manifests in your life, then its purpose is to push you to a higher level of perception. Life always gives us the experiences we need for the evolution of our consciousness; without them, there would be no progress made or awakening to our true self. So, when challenges *do* appear, it's essential to remember that there's always a big picture, and a specific reason for them manifesting. After doing this, you'll realise that all experiences *can* serve the greater good if you're willing to tweak your perspective of them.

Most, however, don't believe they're the creators of their life. Even many who claim they do, don't believe it in their heart of hearts. Their attitude towards challenging situations points out the obvious. The way most people react to unexpected twists and turns is to crumble or project the blame onto someone else or even onto God.

Maybe someone hurt you in the past, and perhaps you've gone some through rough times—we all have. And of course, it's normal to go through unpleasant experiences, as they teach us who we are and help develop our character. It's important to realise, however, that all circumstances are powerless without our reaction to them. Instead of focusing on what people *did* to us, we should focus on what our experiences with them taught us instead. When we shift our perspective, we change our emphasis on the situation. When we do this, we also discover that our perception of the events determines the impact they have on our lives. What happens isn't the issue, as most challenges can be overcome, at least inwardly, if we respond to them correctly. If we're not responding to situations with awareness and understanding that's down to us, and no one else.

Many are afraid to be who they are because they fear rejection from those around them; thus, they give away their power by allowing their opinions to form the basis of their identity. They've been programmed to shun the responsibility for their creative power, as it's always easier to point the finger and blame someone else. Only when one is willing to gaze into the mirror of creation, however, do they realise that what they perceive is a reflection of their state of consciousness.

"Assume full responsibility for the things you observe, and if you do not like what you see, know you have the power to change them. Then exercise that power and you will observe the change you caused. If you are truly willing to assume that responsibility, you are set free."
– Neville Goddard

A great way of realising that you're the creator of your reality is to do this; for one day, keep a watchful eye on your thoughts and the feelings generated by them. You'll see that most of the signs that appear throughout your day have their origin in the ideas that are most predominant in your mind. You're responsible, on some level, for all you experience in this reality as nothing happens by chance. As I wrote before, life always gives you what you need in the present moment. All experiences can be catalysts for the expansion of your consciousness if you define them as such. For this reason alone, it's *illogical* to have a victim mentally as even a tiny shift in perspective can transform you from an unconscious victim into a conscious, and creative victor.

When one understands the nature of physical reality, they realise that all things already exist, in the eternal present. The power of manifestation is the art of consciously shifting to the reality of one's fulfilled desire. Many call this the law of attraction, but I prefer to call it the law of *allowance,* as we simply need to allow all that's in our blueprint to come to us, exactly when it needs to. We achieve this by trusting in divine timing, releasing our resistance to life in the process. Indeed, the only thing keeping our dreams at arm's length is the fact that we're holding onto beliefs that *contradict* our true nature.

"A change of feeling is a change of destiny."
– Neville Goddard

When you desire to shift to a particular reality, the realm of feeling is where the magic happens, as your emotions are the conduit between your thoughts and beliefs. You only feel when you believe something to be true, and as a result, the outer world bends to your perception. It's essential to think *from* the state desired because, in reality, the universe is a library of emotional states we can choose from at any given moment. In the words of Christ: *thy kingdom come, thy will be done, on earth* (physical reality) *as it is in heaven* (our imagination).

"Take me at my word. It is impossible without motion to bring anything into being, and the motion is within you. Knowing exactly what you want, view the world from the premise that you have it. If the world remains the same you haven't moved. Only when it can be seen after the change, can you know you have moved. Now, continue thinking from the new state, for motion can be detected only by a change of position relative to another object. A friend is a good frame of reference. Looking at his face let him see you as he would if your desire were fulfilled. He would see you differently, would he not? If he is one who would congratulate you, accept his congratulations. Extend your hand mentally and feel the reality of his hand. Listen and hear the reality of his words of congratulations. Then have faith in your unseen reality, for if you do, no power can stop it from coming into your world."
–Neville Goddard

Aligning your thoughts and feelings is much easier when you think *from* the state desired and not of it. To be in the state desired is to assume your desire is already a reality. How would you think and feel if you were the person you aspire to be in the here and now? Anchor yourself in that state and allow the universe to guide you into making it a tangible reality. Don't think of *how* you'll get to the reality of your preference as God's ways are not our own, or in other words, the mind isn't designed to know *how* things will come about. We must allow the higher self to take care of the how, while we relax, and focus on the here and now. Christ pointed out man's creative power when he said in the Bible:

"Verily, verily I say unto you, He that believeth on me, the works that I do shall he do also; and greater works than these shall he do; because I go unto my Father."
– John 14:12

To believe in Christ is to believe in yourself, as Christ is our creative power. The Christ sits at the *right hand* of the Father because the right hand of God is the power of manifestation, the human imagination, the conduit between the higher self and the ego.

"Scripture teaches that the power that creates the entire universe is not without man, but within man, as man's own wonderful human Imagination. That is the creative power of the world. All things exist in the human Imagination, so if the word 'God' would turn you out, try to make the adjustment within yourself and begin to believe that the God of Christendom, the Lord Jesus of Christendom, is your own Imagination."
– Neville Goddard

Most have become accustomed to living in anxiety, or have a ton of anger suppressed inside them; is it any wonder why they attract violent situations? If you repress anger, eventually, it's mirrored at you by the people you attract in your reality. Remember, it's *all* you; even the versions of the people you perceive are reflections of your state of consciousness. Any resentment you have against another shows up in your reality sooner rather than later. There's no point in being outwardly kind to someone if you're resenting them within as eventually, all is revealed. Be kind to people in your inner world as it's the origin of every circumstance that appears in your life. Love thy neighbour as thyself because they *are* thyself.

Let's become more aware of our creative potential and lock into our natural state of being. When we do this, the universe has no choice but bring us everything we need in magical and synchronistic ways. In many of the ancient traditions, mystics have correlated the subconscious with the Divine Mother—the womb of creation. Jesus defined the awakened man as the bridegroom. He used this analogy because when you become a conscious creator in your life, nature serves you much like a wife serves her husband. The Divine Mother (subconscious feeling) gives her child anything he believes he can have. The irony is that she did anyway, as the universe never contradicts what you emit via your state of being; making this law conscious, however, works wonders.

MARRIAGE

Marriage is a controversial subject to write about, as most of my readers are probably going to be married. First, let me state that marriage, just like everything else, is a neutral concept, a neutral idea. The only questions that come to mind concerning marriage are, what are your true motivations? Are you married out of love, or out of fear?

Many marry either due to peer pressure from their parents, or because they don't want to be alone. They marry with the motive of avoiding the possibility of dying alone, so they sign themselves up to an agreement written by law that they'll stay tied to the hip of someone, who they can't stand half the time. Why would a person *do* such a thing?

People need to become conscious of how they're creating their reality, and one of the first steps is to *question* their motivations. Marriage has a better chance of being successful if the people involved are willing to merge with the spouse within themselves before, they marry, or they can begin this process if they are already. Otherwise, there's a possibility that desperation and fear-based over co-dependency will taint their union, which ruins all trust and the chance of true love flourishing. I support marriage if the motivates of both partners are pure, and they're rooted in divine love, which is complete freedom sanctioned from both sides. The paradox, however, is that many who are dependent on none for their happiness won't feel inclined to marry unless their soul desires that experience.

Where did the tradition of marriage originate from? Back in ancient times, and particularly in Indian history, for example, political weddings were common, as they would help keep the peace between the royal families that ruled over different regions. The royals desired to keep their bloodline *pure*, so they would either marry from another royal family or in some cases, their relatives. The same year that Tutankhamun of Ancient Egypt became Pharaoh, he married Ankhesenamun, his half-sister, the daughter of Akhenaten and Nefertiti. Fast forward a few thousand years and half the world's population is married, with many regretting that they are. Some of them are unhappy because their parents forced them to wed a stranger. Regardless of the culture, I believe women have the right to decide who they want to marry, and if they even prefer to marry at all. Marriage has become a farce in this respect because it's binding people who aren't in love. It's my firm conviction; nevertheless, these outdated traditions will dissolve the more humanity awakens to its innate divinity.

To me, marriage says little about how much two people love each other. Many couples who aren't married are genuinely in love, while many married couples aren't. Marriage is just a ceremony, and sometimes, the reason people marry is to show off in front of their families and friends.

People should never rush into marriage; they should be in a relationship for at least two or three years so they can use the reflection to help them become more of their authentic selves, first. If used correctly, the relationship can heal them before they make such a big decision. The key to a lasting relationship is for both partners to work *with* the baggage that arises together. In being of assistance to each other when things inevitably do get challenging and most importantly, each partner owning their baggage, then the partnership can thrive. Blaming your partner is the easy way out, rare are those souls who are willing to cease pointing the fingers and gaze in the mirror of creation to see that their challenges belong solely to them.

Marry yourself! Unite the mind with the higher self on a conscious level and then project that wholeness of being onto your partner; show others they're capable of doing it as well through your example. Once you marry yourself, your ideas about marriage might change. You may not desire to tie someone else down any longer as you'll own yourself. Those who want to control others only wish to because they don't know themselves.

Know thyself; become *conscious* of who and what you are. Ask yourself if marriage is truly for you. Honesty is one of the best gifts you can give to yourself and others. If you jump into a wedding when you don't honestly prefer to, then you're not only wasting your time, but your partner's too. The illusion of linear time is one of the most precious things we have as physical beings—use it wisely because life is a lot shorter than you think.

MATURITY

Many quote the cliché that life begins at forty, but I don't agree; life starts when one decides to let go of the fear-based need to control their reality and as a result, live in harmony with existence.

When people reach adulthood, they usually have so many masks glued to their face. Masks they've inherited from those they spent the most time with as they were growing up, such as their parents, siblings and friends. The awakening of true maturity begins when one realises that they aren't being themselves until they cease wearing these masks; they accept themselves as they are, and as a result, reveal their *face* to the world.

"And he said unto another, Follow me. But he said, Lord, suffer me first to go and bury my father. Jesus said unto him, let the dead bury their dead: but go thou and preach the kingdom of God."
– Luke 9:59-60

When one starts to perceive the world through their *own* eyes, rather than through the eyes of others, it can be challenging at first, no doubt. It's like they've hit the reset button on their perception to start all over again. This occurs when the awakening process truly gets underway; one must reprogram themselves from the habits and beliefs they've become accustomed to over the years. To stay true to themselves, they're going to have to drop some of the beliefs and customs prevalent in their society. Christ pointed this out when he said in the Gospel:

"A man's enemies will be members of his own household."
— Matthew 10:36

The above passage is undoubtedly true for those in the purifying fires of the awakening process. Another aspect of maturity is the ability to remain calm and not take the negative opinions of others aimed at oneself personally. Mature people understand that only hurt people hurt others. When a person rises above the hate of another who's testing their resolve, they don't allow their behaviour to define them. To me, this is one of the most significant signs that maturity is developing within a person; with this in mind, there aren't many mature people in the world today. Even many adults still allow the negative opinions of others to define them. We need to redefine the concept of maturity, because many of the issues in the world today stem from people believing they know what's best when, in many cases, they don't.

If society is to progress, adults need to pay those who are younger the same amount of respect they demand from them. Why do some believe that taking advice from a younger person means they're inferior or worthless? This example is just one of countless negative beliefs prevalent in our society that needs to be abolished, because, in truth, age has *nothing* to do with how mature a person is. The more experiences one has in life doesn't necessarily determine whether they'll learn from them or not, as some repeat the same mistakes their entire life. Sadly, many people die without learning what they needed to, only to reincarnate to try all over again.

The quicker one learns, the less they'll have to repeat their mistakes; thus, the more mature they become. The first step one must take in achieving an accelerated state of development is to become familiar with the lies or immaturity within themselves. People should examine themselves daily so they can discern whether the elements within them are aligned with their integrity or not. Maturity, which to me is another word for authenticity, is a process, and it comes in varying degrees. Paradoxically, the more mature one becomes, the more childlike they become; they're able to enjoy their life without the inner resistance that often creates an abundance of unnecessary suffering.

When one's inner world becomes their primary focus, they see just how connected the inner and outer realms are. They realise that they mirror one another meticulously and that its they who are responsible for their perception of the situations that manifest in their lives. Once they take responsibility for the darkness in themselves, then in my eyes, they're becoming mature. It's up to every one of us to deal with our baggage, as we have it for a reason. No more pointing the fingers at others, it's time for us to be who we truly are, and not who everyone else told us we should be.

MEDITATION

When the average person hears the word meditation, the first thing that comes to mind is Buddha sitting with his legs crossed and eyes closed under a tree. While this may be one form of meditation, having such a limited definition attached to their understanding of the practice can prevent them from experiencing the benefits of a meditative lifestyle.

One can train themselves to be in a meditative state while they're doing anything. Mindfulness is a discipline where the practitioner utilises their awareness to live in a meditative state throughout their day. Merging their mind with their body by using their senses to full capacity to focus them in the present, they perform actions in total absorption. Doing this enables the practitioner to enjoy whatever they're doing. The so-called mundane activities of everyday life don't bother the person who can live in that meditative flow. The truth is one can learn how to enjoy almost anything if it's done in the right state of consciousness.

"Meditation is the path which will lead you toward the supreme. Once you start meditating, things around you will start changing. People who are around you will be able to feel that positive energy. Your vibes and aura will start changing and will become more positive."
– Guru Ma, Ritu

Meditation isn't an action, but a state of being. After practising meditation for a while, one realises how effortlessly their life unfolds when they stay in the meditative state. Their mind becomes sharper, their awareness is focused more on the present, and as a result, they're more capable of surrendering the reins of control to the higher self. Only when a person *surrenders*, are they capable of accepting what the present moment contains. One of my favourite forms of meditation is jogging, as it puts me into that flow zone. I feel my body from within while I'm running, and it brings me immeasurable peace.

Even as I write this book, by doing what I love, the performance of this action plunges my consciousness into the still-waters of the present. As I'm writing, most of the time, there aren't any thoughts in my mind, as I've become identified with something deeper than my intellect. In this state, I become the witness as I observe my higher self write the book *through* the conduit of my body. We should follow our passions as often as we can, they are our calling. Krishna, in the Bhagavad Gita, mentioned this state when he said:

"Action is duty, but let not your ego (mind) focus on the fruits of action (It's result) be inwardly non-attached to both action or inaction."
– Bhagavad Gita 2:47

During activity that ignites the fires of bliss in our being, we embody the meditative state. We don't need to *force* ourselves into the present moment. The practice of mindfulness works better when we follow our passion. Living in the present is a *by-product* of following our joy. Life in the present is spontaneous, effortless; this is the meditative lifestyle. Krishna, again points this out in the Gita when he says:

"Through the path of right action alone, Janaka and other karma yogis alike he attained perfection. To be capable of offering right guidance to others, you also, should be active."
– Bhagavad Gita 3:20

The purpose of meditation is to transcend the old self, which enables one to become a conduit for wisdom. Emptiness is meditation; it's a state of consciousness where one is free of thought and emotion while they're anchored in stillness. In this state, one transcends the illusion of linear time, and the fear-based grip the old self has on their consciousness. All the lies, tricks and illusions of the mind are seen through instantly when the sun of pure consciousness rises within oneself. Meditation invokes *clarity* and the reinforcement of who you truly are.

"To the mind that is still, the entire universe surrenders."

– Lao Tzu

Paradoxically, one can also meditate *while* experiencing thoughts and emotions; this is the point of living in a meditative state. When one becomes identified with the deeper level of their being, thoughts and feelings that arise on the surface of the mind are observed with awareness and precision. In becoming the observer to the old self, one no longer allows the illusions to define them, and as a result, integrate them. Working with negative emotions, for example, to identify the beliefs generating them can only be done in a meditative state. One must elevate their awareness above the feeling while allowing it to be there as they pull the misaligned perceptions out the swamp of their unconscious mind.

"One who is able to see the light when they are surrounded by darkness is a true meditator."

– Guru Ma, Ritu

Transcendental meditation is the practice of sitting or lying completely still with one's eyes closed; this is the form of meditation my teacher, *Guru Ma, Ritu* teaches. Profound spiritual experiences are sometimes the by-product of transcending the old self as there are many dimensions hidden within you *beyond* this one. When your cup is empty, it becomes filled with the intoxicating joy, bliss, and peace of the divine; it's then your duty to take your renewed cup of joy out into the world and be a blessing to all around you.

"Create in me a clean heart, O God; and renew a right spirit within me. Cast me not away from thy presence; and take not thy holy spirit from me. Restore unto me the joy of thy salvation; and uphold me with thy free spirit. Then will I teach transgressors thy ways; and sinners shall be converted unto thee."

– Psalm 51: 10-13

When the Bible mentions the word God, it's referring to the higher self, which is your divine self; as it's the version of you that is closer to the source, vibrationally speaking. The soul's blueprint, or in other words, the *will of God*, unfolds when one is in a state of balance between the physical and higher selves. The higher self or super-conscious mind is the God-self within us, and when we align with the higher self, we align with the will of the divine. Yoga (union with the source) is what all the great masters have been teaching since time immemorial. It's only fear-based beliefs that convince people to do things that don't benefit them. The Gita refers to this state in the below passage:

"When the Chitta (feeling, which reflects what one believes to be true) is completely subjugated and is calmly anchored in the Self (Higher Self), the yogi being devoid of attachment to all desires (The outcome of actions), is spoken of as God-united."

– Bhagavad Gita 6:18

Meditation has also been scientifically proven to untangle the nerve cells in the brain that form the old self. Monks and Nuns have had their brains scanned by neuroscientists as they sat in altered states of consciousness invoked by transcendental meditation, prayer and other practices, and the scientists were amazed at what they beheld. Their frontal lobes lit up as brightly as the sun. They were experiencing levels of bliss, peace, and happiness the researchers hadn't witnessed before. Meditation invokes a phenomenon known as *neuroplasticity*, which is the untangling of the nerve cells or hardwiring in the brain, to make space for new synaptic connections to emerge, which promotes conscious change. Meditation, in this sense, is a fire that burns away the old self. Again, in the Gita, this is known as the *Yajna*:

"All karma or effects of actions are completely burned away from the liberated being who, free from attachment, with his mind enveloped in wisdom (the higher self), performs the true spiritual fire rite."

– Bhagavad Gita 4:23

If the children of every nation learned how to meditate at school, it would not only accelerate the development of society, but it would also, eventually, bring world peace and solve many of the challenges we face as a civilisation. The children, who are the future, would have a greater awareness of their true selves and would understand that everyone *is* themselves. Those who know this can never harm another.

A simple method of living in a meditative state more often is to take a moment to pause whatever you're doing to become aware of the natural flow of your breathing. When you feel rushed and chaotic, stop for a moment, close your eyes, and concentrate on your breathing without forcing it. It's important to allow the breath to flow naturally as you hone your awareness in on it. You'll notice as you practice this, that the slower you're breathing, the more relaxed you become. This is because the mind and the breath are intrinsically connected. The breath is your life-force; it's what ties the mind to this dimension, and why your body stops breathing when it dies.

Another practice is to merge your body with your mind as often as you can. What does this mean? Whatever you focus on grows. If your focus is on negative thoughts most of the time, they will keep spinning on the carousel of your mind and controlling the way you feel and behave. When you identify with the subtle energy within your body, you find yourself anchored in the present. The hurricane of thoughts slows down; this is because your focus is no longer on them. Let's say, for example, you're washing the dishes. Instead of rushing through them as most do, wash them a little slower than you usually would. As you hold a plate in your hand, feel your hand from within, you should feel a subtle tingle within it; this is the astral body, and it exists throughout your physical body. When you're able to feel your entire body from within as you perform any action, then you've discovered the peace of God.

"Do one thing at a time and while doing it put your whole soul into it, to the exclusion of all else."
– Swami Vivekananda

The old self often tries to convince you that you're missing something; like you have a big hole in your chest that needs filling by one sensory experience after another. This is the main reason why the mind has so many desires. Most of them are desperate attempts to fill this void it believes is within itself, but no matter how many of its wishes come true, it's *never* satisfied. The core of this issue is just a belief system; people believe they're incomplete when they're already whole in themselves.

"The sense of lack is part of the illusion created by the mind. When you know you are not your mind, then the illusion of lack disappears—no more lack! Nothing is or ever was lacking. The belief that something is lacking makes this seem true, but it is not true. Your beliefs are powerful! You create the experience of lack simply by believing that something is lacking."
– Gina Lake, Ten Teachings for One World

The mind, with its mental and emotional patterns, need to be transcended for you to discover the peace that passeth all understanding. Thoughts and feelings reflect what you believe to be true about yourself or the circumstance at hand. You can have the same thought twice, for example, and not believe it the first time, and as a result, no feeling will arise as you're not allowing it to define you. But, if you have that same thought again and react to it out of fear because you believe it may be true, then you've become identified with it. You must not identify with your old self, as it's not who you are; it's a phantom pretending to be you.

You must discover *why* the thoughts are there, what fears and beliefs they are pointing you towards to begin the process of no longer allowing them to define you.

"For he that is entered into his rest, he also hath ceased from his own works, as God did from his."
– Hebrews 4:10

The goal of meditation is the state of *samadhi*, which is a spiritual ecstasy beyond description. Once you've sipped from the heavenly spring that perpetually gushes out from your soul, then anything the world can offer you through the senses becomes trivial. The intoxication of heavenly bliss is our natural state as we're already one with the divine—we've just forgotten due to the illusory beliefs hijacking our perception.

Once you've tasted ecstasy within, you can bring it out into the world. Your radiance will shine upon the hearts of many, reforming them in the process. We're only at our best when we get beyond the old self, which is a personality we've always defined as ourselves. Meditation helps one accomplish this if done consistently; *alignment* should be the priority of every person.

MIND

The mind is one of the great fascinations of the human experience. Scientists, psychologists, and therapists, to this day, are still baffled by its seemingly infinite complexities; just what *is* the mind?

The mind is an instrument we use to navigate through physical reality, but it isn't limited to just the firings inside our brain; we actually have *two* minds, and not just the one we believe defines us. The two minds are the physical mind, which governs the intellect, habits, memory and the five senses, and the higher self; the nonlinear aspect of our consciousness that orchestrates our life in ways incomprehensible to the ego.

The mind's function is to focus our consciousness in the present moment. The ways of the higher self are, as I just wrote, incomprehensible to the rationale of the physical mind, simply because it's incapable of knowing how the story of our life will unfold. This is why we need to train ourselves to let go of the need to know how things will happen and embrace the unknown, as only the higher self is capable of such feats; drop the how and focus on the here and now.

The higher self communicates to the physical self through one's intuition. When one is calm, they may get a glimpse of a possible future reality—but everything is just that, a *possibility*. Physical reality is fluid and malleable, every choice we make has the potential to take us to a different timeline with a different outcome; no future events are set in stone.

The old self is an aspect of the physical mind, but as I wrote in the ego chapter, it is not one's true individuality. The ego structure is a blank canvas that can be reset and repainted at any time. The personality is the *mask* our consciousness wears in this cosmic drama; this is why the definition of the Greek word persona is mask:

A persona (plural personae or personas), in the word's everyday usage, is a social role or a character played by an actor. The word is derived from Latin, where it originally referred to a theatrical mask. The Latin word probably derived from the Etruscan word "phersu", with the same meaning, and that from the Greek πρόσωπον (prosōpon)

– Wikipedia

Through the focus of the mind, we have a perspective as a physical being, and this is the point of having an ego, as it gives us that spark of individuality no other can replicate. This mask goes hand in hand with the illusion of separation from the source and each other. Not all illusions are inherently negative, as this one enables us to have an individual perspective as we play the game of life.

We are one with the divine, as it is the very *substance* of existence. If we weren't, we wouldn't exist, it's as simple as that. God isn't someone or something separate from us; the majority of people believe so, when, in fact, it's the force keeping them alive.

The higher self is beyond linear space-time, and its role is to guide us through the physical realm, as it can see the big picture. The thinking mind is said to be blind, as it's only capable of perceiving what's happening in the present moment, or what happened in the past without the higher self's guidance. Sometimes, it filters what's happening in the present *through* the eyes of past experiences. Just like your eyes are subject to the physical realm, they can't perceive that which is beyond it, so too, can the mind only perceive the trails it's left behind or the here and now.

The foundation of all great masters' teachings is to *be here now* for this reason. When one is in the present without the illusions of the past distorting their perception of it, they're using their mind correctly. Peace reigns supreme in the temple of their being when they let go of what was and accept what is. When the higher self takes the reins, it leads one to the Promised Land the divine intended for them when it breathed life into their consciousness.

In the Hindu epic, the *Mahabharata*, we see an example of the roles of the physical mind and higher self in the allegory of the royal brothers, Dhritarashtra and Pandu. Dhritarashtra was born *blind*; he represents the physical mind, and his brother Pandu, whose name means *white*, represents the higher self.

Firstly, Pandu is the king of Hastinapura (physical reality) and as a result of him (the higher self) being on the throne; the kingdom thrives and flourishes (without resistance). To make an extremely long story *short*, eventually, Pandu dies, and the only person available to take his place as ruler is his blind brother. When the blind Dhritarashtra becomes king, chaos breaks out everywhere, not only in the city of Hastinapura but also within the royal house itself (the body in resistance). The kingdom eventually becomes divided, which culminates in a monstrous war between the sons of Pandu and Dhritarashtra in which almost every member of the royal family is slain. Dhritarashtra was counselled many times to give up the crown, and consequently, the throne (control of physical reality on an ego level) not only by his wife Gandhari, but his uncle Bhishma, but he was too afraid to let go.

Just like the blind Dhritarashtra wouldn't give up his control of Hastinapura out of fear, many have an ego that believes it's in control of its reality and that it belongs on the throne, but this isn't the purpose of the blind mind. Dhritarashtra was controlling the kingdom out of fear; he was constantly looking over his shoulder because he believed his family were plotting to take the crown away from him. My point in bringing up this ancient allegory is that until one learns how to *trust* their higher self, by flowing with everything that it manifests for them in the unknown, their kingdom will be in jeopardy. The physical mind isn't capable of functioning in the ways the higher self does. When one lives without resistance by accepting everything as it comes because they know everything happens for a specific reason, they're trusting in their higher self.

In the science of Astrology, this dynamic can also be seen in the polarity of the signs *Gemini* and *Sagittarius*; with Gemini or the 3rd house representing the physical mind, and Sagittarius or the 9th house representing the higher self. To function as a whole being, one must use both minds in tandem by using each correctly. This state of balance is union with the true self; it can only be realised when both minds become one. This is what the term *mindfulness* actually means; it doesn't mean to have a mind full of content, it means to bring both minds in unison, thus, it becomes whole, and a channel for the wisdom of the soul.

> *"Rule your mind, or it will rule you."*
> *– Buddha*

This state of wholeness, Yoga, Zen, or whatever you prefer to call it is our true nature. To realise your wholeness of being is the key to living in a state of balance. In this state, you use your imagination consciously and creatively by trusting in the intuitive guidance of the higher self. The higher self loves the unknown, and it urges you to embrace it. Your nonlinear self has left your physical self many clues there; do you have the courage to go look for them?

The physical mind is an extraordinary instrument. We've not tapped into its full potential yet. The power of thought is what separates us from other intelligent forms of life in this world. Many on the spiritual path incorrectly assume that to be present, we need to go thoughtless all day. I say this respectfully, but if we sat around all day without thought, even though it would feel good to escape from the turmoil that's often between our ears, we'd get nothing done! As I keep saying throughout this book, *balance* is required. You're a person and a soul—so be both! Use the power of thought consciously and creatively. Divine inspiration infuses our thoughts when we're in the correct state to receive it. Don't fall for the spiritual superego trap by believing all thoughts are limiting; it's only your belief in the involuntary thoughts that reflect your subconscious self-sabotaging tendencies that cause you problems.

We have around 70,000 thoughts per day, and most of them are automatic and repetitive; you shouldn't allow them to disturb you. The technique of witnessing your thoughts is useful if you use it to discover where the ideas come from, and why you have them between your ears. Becoming *familiar* with the old self and its patterns is the point of observing it.

To be the observer doesn't imply being passive and allow the resistance to happen as you watch; this does nothing but reinforce your tendencies. You need to work *with* the resistance to dissolve it by observing your mind with awareness and curiosity. It's crucial to explore the ideas and the feelings that come along with them to see what they're attempting to show you. Emotions reflect your perception of the environment. You must go into your fear-based feelings to become aware of the beliefs hijacking your perception when you're triggered.

The key to self-mastery is understanding how the mind works, and that our perspectives determine how we think and feel. Once you master the mind, creation becomes your servant. You can then *play* with physical reality and bring into manifestation anything that comes from the depths of your heart.

So, trust in your higher self; it knows what you don't, it can see what you can't see, and the unknown is known to the greater thee. Once you allow the mind to accept its job of focusing you in the present without resistance, then you'll experience new levels of joy, peace, synchronicity, compassion and love for all of existence.

MONEY

Since time immemorial, religious teachers have drilled the belief that the love of money is the root of all evil into the heads of the masses. Money, however, is neutral like everything else in physical reality, as it's an energy people can utilise positively or negatively. Wealth is defined by many as the cause of the suffering we see on a global scale, but I don't see it that way. The limiting beliefs that generate the greed and apathy in those who aren't willing to share their resources are what's perpetuating the hunger, poverty and famine we see worldwide. The super-rich, the billionaires, could easily end third-world poverty, but they don't want to. We live in a capitalist society where everything is money-based; from the media to the news, to fossil fuels, the list is endless. We even have to *pay* to use the restroom in some public places now.

There's nothing wrong with desiring abundance in the form of money, as we need it to live, to travel, and buy food, for example. Having money can help us achieve what we need to as it enables us to explore the world and to help others in ways that aren't possible without it. Some are completely attached to their wealth, however, and strive to earn more, even though they have more than they're capable of spending in their lifetime.

"I'm not saying we shouldn't have money, I need money to pay rent, I need money to buy clothes, to buy food and do the normal things of life, I'm not denying that. But to fall in love with money, and to want money for money's sake is simply a false concept of power."

– Neville Goddard

Money is one form of abundance, but there are others such as health, gifts, loving relationships, creativity, and our connection to the source, with the latter being the greatest. Yoga (union with the divine) is our natural state, and the joy of being connected is the only form of abundance that can't perish; as we're eternally *one* with the source. The peace of God is always there, waiting for us to tap into it. When we make this connection conscious, life rewards us for doing so. Surrender brings *all else unto you*, exactly when you need it; this is what Christ was referring to when he said:

"Lay not up for yourselves treasures upon earth, where moth and rust doth corrupt, and where thieves break through and steal: But lay up for yourselves treasures in Heaven, where neither moth nor rust doth corrupt, and where thieves do not break through nor steal: For where your treasure is, there will your heart be also."

– Matthew 6:19-21

This treasure in heaven will always be within you. You can never lose it; even if it feels as if you have, you simply need to *access* the stillness in the core of your being. Once you know how to access your soul, you'll realise that there's something dwelling inside of you that puts anything the world can offer you to shame, the kingdom of God.

"But seek ye first the kingdom of God, and his righteousness; and all these things shall be added unto you."

– Matthew 6:33

The paradox is that seeking God first can also bring about great material prosperity, as our state of being creates our reality. So, if one is anchored in the peace of the divine, filled with faith that the higher self will provide them with what they need, they'll effortlessly manifest opportunities to bring money into their lives.

"'Few mortals know that the kingdom of God includes the kingdom of mundane fulfilments,' Babaji observed. 'The divine realm extends to the earthly, but the latter, being illusory, cannot include the essence of reality."

– Mahavatar Babaji, Autobiography of a Yogi

I don't see anything wrong in being well-off financially as long as one is willing to help the less fortunate, and they don't allow their identity to be defined by their wealth. If a person can be happy while they're broke, they can be satisfied whenever they want, as their state of being isn't dependent on their finances. In the Gospel, Christ was confronted by a rich young man who asked how he could attain the kingdom of heaven; Jesus responded by saying:

"If thou wilt be perfect, go and sell that thou hast, and give to the poor, and thou shalt have treasure in heaven: and come and follow me. But when the young man heard that saying, he went away sorrowful: for he had great possessions."
– Matthew 19:21-22

Christ wasn't against the fact that he had money like some erroneously believe. He told him to sell all he had because he unconsciously defined himself *through* his wealth. He was enslaved by his riches, as his state of being was dependent on it. Jesus counselled the youngster to sell everything he owned so he could be free of this illusion. Everything experienced through the senses only brings momentary gratification; it always fades. Money can only purchase things subject to creation and the senses; thus, it can *never* become a source of true happiness. Krishna was referring to the transitory nature of physical reality when he said in the Gita:

"O Son of Kunti, the experience of heat and cold, pleasure and pain, are produced by the senses with their objects. All of these are limited as they are subject to a beginning and an end. They are transitory, O Descendant of Bharata: be patient!"
– Bhagavad Gita 2:14

Seek your worth in the core of your being and nowhere else; your essence *is* one with the infinite consciousness that conceived us into existence. Discovering your worth through your connection to the source detaches you from creation; thus, the fear of loss dissolves. When you define yourself through external stimuli, such as in relationships, money, or addictive substances, for example, fear strikes when there's any chance of loss. Freedom lies in discovering the peace that isn't dependent on what happens to you. Once you tap into the source, you realise you're the director of this drama rather than a member of the audience, who in most cases, wholly define themselves *through* the senses. Whether you have money or not, you can be happy and at peace, as embodying your natural state is ultimately a *decision*. You're whole within yourself already; you just *believe* the opposite. When your happiness isn't dependent on what happens, you'll attract the forms of abundance encoded in the blueprint of your soul. You'll also realise that you *are* abundance and that you're the wealthiest being in creation, as you're the *only* being in existence; thus, you already own everything.

MOTIVATIONS

When it comes to doing the right thing, our motives are everything. People must check their motivations before making any big decision in life. Motivations are formed by beliefs, whether one's conscious of them or not, as people always feel motivated to do what they *believe* serves them best, at any given moment. Thus, it's safe to say that one's motivations reflect their perception of themselves and life as a whole.

When a person has selfish motives influencing them, it's because fear-based beliefs are hijacking their perception. Let's say, for example, a person gets into a relationship, not out of love, but out of desperation and anxiety. The fear of being alone drives them; their motive is to *use* another as a means of security. What would they have to believe to generate such motivations? Maybe they don't think they're capable of making it on their own? Perhaps they believe being single makes them worthless? Maybe their definition of being alone is out of whack? They may not love themselves enough to enjoy their own company or trust that life will bring them the right person, at the right time? Perhaps they don't trust in the way their life is unfolding? The list of potential limiting beliefs is endless! Through this example alone, you can see why it's essential to fish these beliefs out of the unconscious. The more aware you become of the old self, the easier time you'll have in transcending its redundant processes.

Most of the time, you need not force things to happen in life. When a person comes to understand the roles of the physical mind and the higher self, they realise that forcing things out of fear or anxiety hardly ever works. People crash face-first into brick walls when they allow the impulses of their conditioning to override the guidance of the higher self. Unfortunately, this is the most common way of finally getting it for most. The pain they experience by being misaligned prods them into the realisation of who they are. This need not be the case, however, they can avoid these brick walls, if they know *when* to act by attuning to their intuition. To do this, bringing their motivations into awareness is key. Before acting on an impulse, search for any fear-based motives generating them. If you manage to find any, you may perceive, ahead of yourself, the primrose path the erroneous beliefs were attempting to lure you down.

Now, this is tricky because not all fear-based motives are negative. For example, being a single parent and having no job may motivate you out of fear of not being able to provide for your children, so you do all you can to find a job to enable you to provide for them. Discernment is crucial—make sure you're doing the right thing. As you see in this example, using fear to motivate you sometimes *can* be helpful.

"Listen unto me carefully Arjuna! That which is spoken of in the scriptures as renunciation is the exact same thing as yoga; for that man who has not renounced selfish motivations can never be a yogi!"
–Bhagavad Gita 6:2

A yogi is one who utilises scientific methods of meditation and introspection to experience union with the divine. According to the Gita, one cannot be a yogi if selfish motives dictate their behaviour. Our natural state is joy, but we can't embody it if we're buying into erroneous beliefs that colour our perception.

The same is also true for any redundant habit you're struggling to shake off. All behaviour, as I've mentioned a few times in this book, is governed by your perception. Habits are subconscious processes that become effortless due to the repetition of the actions associated with them. For one to truly let these patterns go, they're going to have to be motivated correctly, because even though these actions are automatic and subconscious, they are still, on some level, a choice.

To free yourself from the desire to wallow in these automatic processes is to discover the reasons why you *believe* perpetuating them is a better alternative than change. You may have unhealthy eating habits, for example, and even though you know that it isn't good for you to eat in such a manner, you can't seem to help yourself. You must investigate your perception to find out why there's a lack of self-love that drives you to perpetuate habits that are detrimental to your wellbeing.

Many struggle with their habits because they lack *motivation*. Even though they say they genuinely want change, they don't seem to want it enough. I know change can be difficult and even scary at times because to change, one must step outside the comfort zone of their familiar feelings to embrace the unknown. The option of reverting into the same patterns, into the comfort zone is always there, but let me tell you that life truly begins where your comfort zone ends.

What matters the most to you in life? What is your passion? When you have clarity on what *matters*, then you'll be more motivated and inspired to take action. Passion is the *key* ingredient to a successful life. A life without it isn't worth living.

If you're unsure about your passion or there's confusion in your mind, then spend time in solitude. Self-reflective times are essential to finding what truly matters, inspires, and motivates you to better yourself daily. Do what sets your soul ablaze so that all who encounter you are enlightened by its flames.

NONATTACHMENT

In the eastern faiths such as Hinduism, Sikhism, Buddhism and Jainism, the practice of nonattachment is taught as a shortcut to enlightenment, but what is it exactly? Many misunderstand what it means to be nonattached. In modern-day India, it's common to see wandering sadhus (renunciants) walking around homeless by choice and in some cases completely naked, not owning any material possessions, outwardly displaying their *apparent* nonattachment.

"Detachment is not that you should own nothing. But that nothing should own you."

– Ali ibn Abi Talib

There have been a few cases where a westerner has renounced all they have to go and live in a cave, believing they'll become free of their challenges. When a few months of staring at cave walls all day and eating leaves pass by, they wind up returning home, devastated and embarrassed. Giving up worldly possessions is a valid path if that's where the higher self is guiding you. *Escapism*, however, isn't the true meaning of nonattachment, as you can enjoy the world and be nonattached; in fact, it's the *only* way you can truly enjoy life. Lord Krishna is a perfect example of someone living in the world, engaged with society without allowing transitory circumstances to define him:

"Even wise men act according to the tendencies of their own nature. All living creatures live according to their Nature; what can suppression truly avail?"

– Bhagavad Gita 3:33

Luminous beings such as Christ and Krishna, realised the final yogic state of *Nirvikalpa Samadhi*; thus, lived permanently in a state of balance. They flowed with the synchronicity that manifested in their lives while embracing the unknown with an unshakable confidence in the divine plan. Their actions were free of selfish motives, and the love in their hearts guided them to their destiny.

> *"Act without expectation."*
> – *Lao Tzu*

Renunciation and nonattachment are intrinsically connected. To renounce the world isn't merely to let go of all worldly possessions; it's to dissolve the components in the mind which convince you to act out of anxiety instead of love, peace, and divine inspiration. Nonattachment is a *by-product* of the letting go of the old self. Once you've integrated your beliefs into knowing to a certain extent, you'll no longer allow transitory situations to determine your state of being. Instead, your connection to the source will define you; thus, you'll go beyond identifying with illusions and be established in the truth. Even some of Christ's disciples realised this state, and this is what he meant when he said in the Gospel:

> *"They are not of the world, even as I am not of the world."*
> – *John 17:16*

The only thing you need to renounce is the illusion of the past. Once you realise that you create your perception of your past experiences *from* the present, you'll be able to redefine the memories that bother you and close the timelines associated with them.

When you embrace the present moment in its totality, you drop your expectations on the outcome of whatever you're doing. Nonattachment isn't something you decide to do with the mind by telling yourself you're going to be detached—it's a natural *by-product* of living in your essence, which isn't in the world, nor of it.

"This kind of person has no purpose of gain in this world with his actions, nor does he lose anything by not performing actions. He's not dependent on anyone for anything."

–Bhagavad Gita 3:18

Nonattachment occurs when you cease allowing transitory circumstances to define you. You're whole within yourself already; you just believe the opposite. The source is *within* you. The unconditional love and bliss of the divine, which is your true self, can't be tarnished by transitory experiences. What do I mean? The core of your being is perpetually blissful and radiating peace—that can *never* change. The issue is that many don't know how to *access* it; they live wholly defined by their body. Living solely through the senses creates much bondage to the outer world, as one seeks their identity in creation, rather than the blissful abode of the creator within.

"No weapon can pierce the self, no fire can burn it; no water can moisten it; nor can any wind wither it. The self is incomparable; it cannot be burnt or wetted or dried. The self is immutable, all-permeating, ever calm, and immovable-forever the same."

– Bhagavad Gita 2:23-24

Only when you're connected to the inner self can truly enjoy what life has to offer you. For example, if you're in an intimate relationship, and before you met your partner, you were already content and happy being alone; there will be no fear of loss degrading the relationship. If your motivations were impure while you were seeking a partner, however, then you'll be afraid of losing them because you were unhappy while you were single. It's most likely that you're using your partner as a source of happiness to cover up your wounds, or in other words, your identity is dependent upon what happens in the relationship.

You can only enjoy something when there's no fear of losing it. The fear of loss causes people so much pain because they're dependent on what they're afraid of losing for their happiness. There's nothing inherently *wrong* in experiencing the fear of loss; however, if that's where you are in your process, then it's where you are, all is well.

The fear of loss teaches us how to stop defining ourselves through the outer world when we're willing to work with it rather than resist it. Fear and pain prod us within to discover a deeper reality, but people only look inside themselves when they're ready.

Christ taught that the kingdom of heaven is *within* you. What he meant is that the only real source of eternal joy is within yourself, and nowhere else. Don't seek permanent joy in things that are impermanent in nature! Cease allowing the impulses of the old self to control you; control them! Discipline yourself by your own standards and conquer the world from your centre. You can only enjoy the world when you no longer seek your identity through it; be in the world but *not* of it.

PLAYFULNESS

Life is a game; even though it seems so *real* to the mind, we're living in a cosmic simulation, a dream. The point of a physical life is for us to experience it from the perspective of the ego and the soul simultaneously. We're only capable of enjoying it, however, when we lighten up and define it as a game, a drama, or a play. When we don't take it all too seriously, we perceive reality through the eyes of the soul. Too many lose sight of this; they believe their life must be defined as a battle or a struggle. To believe you must endure life, however, means that you're defining it in a way that doesn't work for you. We're here to *thrive*, not merely to survive.

"Presiding over the (physical) mind and the senses of hearing, sight, touch, taste and smell, The Blessed Lord enjoys the sensory world."
— *Bhagavad Gita 15:9*

The divine consciousness enjoys all manifestations *through* us. The source resides in the hearts of all, and its plan is for us to become one with our higher selves. By forming a conscious connection with the nonlinear aspect of your consciousness, peace, health, and prosperity manifest as a by-product of the state, which is known by the rishis of Ancient India as *yoga*—union with the divine. One of the many names of Sri Krishna is *Parampurusha;* which means the supreme enjoyer.

There's no doubt that life can be unpleasant, and of course, there are times when we forget who we are, and lose sight of the big picture. Challenging circumstances will always bring us down in vibration until we redefine them. Learning how to define life as a game is a process in of itself because, for decades, you've most likely taken it far too seriously. It's time to *rewire* this node in the maze of your mind, because, without any form of opposition, you'd be seeking forever and would never find.

Imagine that you're fifteen years old and you've been waiting months for a video game to be released. You've been looking forward to it for ages—your friends at school talk about it every day, and you're saving up your pocket money to buy it. The day the game is released, you go to the store, purchase it, and bring it home. Upon first playing the game, you fly through it so quickly that you beat it within just five hours. You waited so long for a game that took only five hours to finish; you'd most likely be disappointed as it was simply too easy. The same could be said about life; if there was no pressure that prods you into the realisation of who you really are, then you'd be bored. Imagine watching a movie and there was no opposition for the protagonist to overcome; you'd be snoring within half an hour!

In this drama, we call life, our ego is the character, and the higher self is the director. Every person on this planet is a masterpiece created by the divine; unfortunately, many don't believe they are. They only wear a mask society pressured them into wearing. Until you wear the right mask, however, you won't step into the role the source intended you to play when it created you. But even the experience of wearing the wrong mask adds to the excitement and the drama; all is well, *trust* in the timing you discover the true self.

"God has given you one face and you make yourself another."
– William Shakespeare

Overcoming life's challenges is the point of this incarnation. We're playing the game of self-discovery amidst the depths of darkness, separation and illusions. You need not define it in a way that makes you feel as if you need to endure it. Train your mind to see this process as a game you're playing. Your true self is hiding behind the cobwebs of your most limiting of beliefs.

Every time you discover a fear-based belief hijacking your perception; you've *levelled up*. You move a step closer to your true self when you bring into consciousness, the unconscious perceptions that convince you to self-sabotage. Learn to have fun with this process. I know it may be challenging initially, but eventually, it will become easier not to take the old self so seriously. In achieving a degree of indifference towards your conditioning, you'll be more capable of transcending its automatic processes.

When you lighten up on yourself, you become more open to change. As a result of you becoming more malleable, so does your life, as your reality is a *projection* of your state of being. As you seek your identity through your connection to the source in your heart, instead of transient circumstances, you play the game in a nonattached state. You also come to realise that nothing that manifests in the outer world can change what you *know* you are in the depths of your soul—a child of the infinite spirit. In identifying with the treasure innate to the depths of your being, there will be no fear of loss; how could you possibly lose anything when you've realised, you're one with all that is? In having this realisation, you'll be more willing and able to *flow* with the tides of life, rather than attempting to swim against its currents.

Now, just because you know on a soul level that you don't really lose anything, it doesn't mean your personality won't mourn when those you love transition into the next world. If you need to grieve because a loved one passed or a relationship or friendship dissolved then, by all means, do so. Don't try and be *super-spiritual* by attempting to suppress your humanity; your pain is beautiful. We're here to be human and divine at the same time—let those tears out. As you identify with the deeper aspect of yourself, emotions feel like ripples on the surface of your being. You'll always feel pain when you lose those close to you as a person; it adds to the drama. Allow it to teach you what it needs to.

"The game of life is a game of boomerangs. Our thoughts, words and deeds return to us sooner or later with astounding accuracy."
— *Florence Scovel Shinn*

Like any game, physical reality has rules we've agreed to abide by before incarnating here. When we become aware of these universal laws, then we're more likely to be successful while playing the game. The main rule of the game is the law of *cause and effect*, which means life is always reflecting our state of being. Our perception holds incredible power, as it determines what we get out of the circumstances that manifest in our lives.

In becoming *conscious* of this law, and sowing the seeds of your preference, you're able to play the game with conscious *intention* instead of random impulsivity. You need to tame your imagination; however, as you're just as capable of creating hell for yourself and others as you are heaven.

Everyone's already creating their reality, they're already playing the game, but unfortunately, most aren't conscious of this fact. They're playing the game unconsciously, but how can one be successful in a game they don't know they're playing? All successful people have a positive and dynamic attitude. They understand that everything starts with their *mindset*. They sow the seeds of success in their mind and are rewarded through the circumstances their optimism brings into manifestation.

"Ye shall know them by their fruits. Do men gather grapes of thorns, or figs of thistles?"
— *Matthew 7:16*

I'll go on record by stating that this is one of the most important chapters in this book. To *play* with physical reality is the entire point of being here. We came to earth to have fun, to enjoy the gift the divine has bestowed upon us, so that it may enjoy it *through* us. Many are looking at their life in a way that doesn't serve them. People must wake up to the reality that this transitory experience is a simulation they've agreed to partake in on a level of consciousness their mind can't comprehend. The source created the universe to enjoy its creation. You can play the role of a victor or a victim in this cosmic drama; the choice is yours.

POWER

All power is borrowed, and so is our time on Earth. Everyone defines power differently; some see money as power, others see it as a high position in a line of employment or the ability to dominate and manipulate people—I could go on forever. The true source of power doesn't come through the transitory world, as everything in it has a beginning and an end. The source is *within* you. All the energy you believe is your own is but a drop in the ocean of the infinite consciousness.

Many wealthy people believe they're powerful because they have an endless supply of money. Media outlets influence the masses through fear-based propaganda, but if you have to manipulate others to get what you want, then it's the complete *opposite* of power. Only the weak feel the need to take advantage of the shortcomings of others.

Tyrannical monarchs are known to have existed all throughout history. Many abused their God-given power and brought terror to their subjects under the belief that they're better than everyone else because they're royalty. These people forgot, however, that it was the divine who put them there in the first place. As its representative, it's their duty to open themselves up as a conduit for wisdom while in such a lofty position. Through the exploitation of the karmic law, many of these rulers had an unpleasant ending to their reigns; man *reaps* what he sows.

"Nearly all men can stand adversity, but if you want to test a man's character, give him power."
– *Abraham Lincoln*

Nowadays, many erroneously believe *fame* is power. They think being a celebrity or having a large following on social media gives them a sense of authority, but the transitory nature of this world impacts even the credibility of movie or pop stars. Their reputations go up and down; if they make even just one mistake, the paparazzi jump on their backs, giving them a bad name for doing something that the reporters are probably guilty of doing themselves. Celebrities hardly ever get any solitude; to me that is one of the *biggest* hells. Be careful what you wish for.

Money is another illusion of power. Don't misunderstand me; there's nothing wrong with desiring it to help you do the things you want such as travelling, for example, but to define money as a source of power is an illusion, as it will *never* make you permanently happy. Sure, you'll be satisfied for a while when you buy the new shoes or the sports car, but eventually, the cracks of dissatisfaction you papered over with your material possessions return. Many billionaires and Hollywood actors have admitted that their wealth and time in the spotlight failed to provide them with the soul-filling satisfaction they so craved.

"So do not fear, for I am with you; do not be dismayed, for I am your God. I will strengthen you and help you; I will uphold you with my righteous right hand."
– Isaiah 41:10

In the Bible, Christ is defined as the creative power and wisdom of God. You draw your creative power directly from the infinite well of the source in the Quantum Field. The hand of the divine consciousness is present in everything that manifests in your life. To seek power outside yourself is to allow the outer world to define you. If you're to be at peace, never let the transitory world dictate your state of being! Embody the true self—it's your point of power as it's only in that state do you have access to divine wisdom and inspiration.

It's humbling to realise that without the source, we're powerless, in fact, without the divine, we wouldn't exist. The higher self knows what we don't; it can see what we can't see. The divine has all pieces of the puzzle together, while each of us are but a piece. True humility is to realise that we're simply *conduits* for the infinite consciousness to express itself in this reality. Pride and vanity dissolve when one knows the source works *through* them when they're in harmony with life.

When you look within, you discover nothing but stillness however, it is *through* that stillness, that you *merge* with the infinite. You become conscious of the fact that you're one with all that is, was and ever will exist. It's through your connection to the collective that you realise your God-given power. Love unites *all* things; it's the glue that binds the multiverse together. The awakening soul also realises that love is the most powerful force in creation; God *is* love.

Strength, courage, awareness, peace, abundance, clarity, forgiveness, wisdom, love, and creativity come from the source. Don't seek anything else before establishing a conscious connection with its infinite intelligence. Seek ye *first* the kingdom of God, and all else shall be added unto you.

You may be physically strong, have an infinite reservoir of money or be a global superstar. You could be an artist and have sold millions of your works worldwide, but verily I say unto thee, that unless you put the source first, then all you've achieved will be in vain; what goes up *must* come down again.

"Yea, though I walk through the valley of the shadow of death, I will fear no evil: for thou art with me; thy rod and thy staff they comfort me."

– Psalm 23:4

To know the divine is to become conscious of your greater self. The higher self is God's *version* of you, and you merge with it by surrendering the old self's attempts to manipulate the story of your life. The old self believes it's in control, that it runs the show in the transitory valleys of physical reality. But, as you walk through the valley of this transient world, you don't get anywhere until you give up trying to control it on the level of the physical mind. The paradox is that you only gain any real sense of control when you hand the reins over to the nonlinear aspect of your being—who sees the big picture.

The source designed the higher self to guide the ego *through* the experience of physical reality. Allow this higher octave of yourself to make all important decisions for you via your intuition. When you learn to flow with whatever life presents you with from moment to moment, then you're no longer fighting yourself. Resistance to life equates to resistance to the guidance of the higher self.

Life always gives you what you *need*, regardless of what you want. Most of your desires are the result of the fear-based motivations generated by limiting beliefs in your unconscious. Discernment is essential; always ask yourself *why* you want what you say you want.

Nothing happens by chance. Trust in the way your life is unfolding and learn to be at peace with the knowledge that you're never given a challenge the divine doesn't know you're capable of overcoming. Let it be and retreat inwardly for the answers you seek. Nothing in the world can bring you eternal joy or happiness. Once you truly realise this, many of your desires will fall away from thee, much resembling the leaves of an autumn tree.

Process

The spiritual path is a *process*, as we're only capable of experiencing life one moment at a time. So many people beat themselves up because they've yet to let go of their fears, habits, and beliefs. If you're one of these people, then you need to trust in the process because nothing goes away until it's taught you what it needs to teach you.

Everything happens *when* it needs to in life. However, this doesn't mean you should be lethargic and stay stuck in the same patterns by choice. You should do all you can to try and change for the better and improve yourself daily if you feel it's necessary. What I'm saying is that you shouldn't beat yourself up or believe you're a failure just because you fall at times, we all do. It doesn't matter how many times you fall, however, only that you get back up again!

In the Hindu epic, the *Mahabharata*, in which the Bhagavad Gita is merely a chapter, Arjuna, who chose Krishna to be his charioteer on the eve of the battle between truth and untruth asked Krishna to drive his chariot between the opposing armies. The Gita is an allegory, obviously; the war of Kurukshetra, (even though some historians believe the war did happen), is symbolic of the war that occurs within oneself when the awakening process gets underway.

Arjuna, who was known to be the ace-archer of his time, became discouraged when he saw his relatives on the opposing army's side. Trembling in fear and disbelief, he dropped his bow and sat in dejection. *"Why must I kill my relatives to find true happiness?"* he asked his charioteer and master, Sri Krishna, who responded by saying:

"O Partha (Son of Kunti, Arjuna), don't surrender to such unmanliness; it is unbecoming to thee. O Scorcher of Foes, forsake this small weakheartedness! Arise!"

– Bhagavad Gita 2:3

I'm sure there have been many times we've all felt like Arjuna as he stood between both armies and beheld his uncles, great uncles, brothers, cousins and teachers arrayed before him, eager for battle. He didn't wish to kill his own flesh and blood (his family on the opposing side being *symbolic* of the inner tendencies and habits we become accustomed to over the years) and dropped his bow in discouragement.

Krishna, allegorically representing the soul or the true self, however, encourages Arjuna to *fight*. We must never give up on the spiritual path, which is an everlasting process to self-mastery. The verse above points this out wonderfully, that no matter how many times you drop your bow, or fall to a bad habit, pick up your Gandiva (bow of determination and self-control), stand up, O Scorcher of Foes (bad habits) and keep going!

We learn from our mistakes more than anything else. All great fighters or tennis players, for example, learn hardly anything when they win, but much when they lose. Losing and winning are two sides of the same coin. As you no longer identify with your actions but become the transcendental witness *beyond* the senses, you attain the state of even-mindedness and transcend duality altogether. In this state, outer circumstances no longer control the way you think and feel.

The awakening process is the entire point of experiencing life in physical reality. In the higher spheres or lesser density realms of the astral and causal planes, for example, time doesn't exist in the same manner that it does here. The experience of progressively unveiling the darkness that eclipses your divinity isn't possible from those higher perspectives. This is why you came down in vibration to Earth, to *play* this game.

The game of life is a gift granted to us by the divine. Many aren't having fun in the game, though, as they define their life as a struggle, or as something they must *endure*. When people label their life as a struggle, then the universe, which has no choice but to reflect what they believe to be true, says: *"Okay! If it's a struggle you desire, then it's a struggle you'll get!"* The outer world responds to our state of being—we always see things as a reflection of our state of consciousness; this is what Christ meant when he said in the Gospel:

"Ask, and it shall be given you; seek, and ye shall find; knock, and it shall be opened unto you."
– *Matthew 7:7*

So, see your awakening process as a game; have *fun* with your baggage, your fears, and unconscious perceptions. Fear-based beliefs resemble children that lie to you about your true nature; laugh at their shenanigans. Learn to work *with* the resistance that prevents you from moving forward with your life, in a playful, child-like manner.

In a playful state, it's much easier to be the person you prefer. When you fall in vibration and start projecting blame onto others, and onto God, the reality around you becomes inert, thus, unchangeable. The secret of transformation is to *play* with reality rather than just experiencing the dual-bound stimuli that impresses your senses.

Waves upon waves of the residual baggage from your past experiences progressively come up for you to deal with during your awakening process. It's a good thing the baggage comes up in waves, a few beliefs or fears at a time because if it all came up in one go, it would most likely *kill* you!

Every time you make even the slightest *conscious* change to your perception and embrace the present without resistance, you've levelled up! One step at a time, you're moving into the direction of your destiny.

If you've taken a backward step in life, this *can* be redefined and used to your benefit if you're willing to take two steps forward. People who relapse into a drug or alcohol addiction, for example, do so with more awareness than they had when they were first addicted. We often fall back into old states and patterns because there's a valuable piece of information that can only be obtained in such a state that we need to take with us into the future. In this sense, there are *no* backwards steps in life, but only if you're willing to make the changes required and climb yourself out of your self-created hole. All things *can* serve a purpose if you tweak your perception of them.

In opening your mind, more treasure ye shall find, sometimes to go forward, we need to rewind. To see what we forgot, to learn what we need, the process is the entire point, listen unto me carefully; take heed! No need to beat yourself up, you've done that enough, you're not a victim to your own power, living in such a way is rough! Enjoy your life, work *with* the contrast, and I promise you that you'll be free from the illusions of the past.

So, *accept* where you are in your process. Do you believe you should be perfect by now? Do you think you should be enlightened or not have any challenges? Many suffer because they have so many expectations that transcend their capabilities. A bit of *realism* is needed here. You're already perfect the way you are because every masterpiece ever created required a process to become one. The Mona Lisa, for example, was only half painted at one time; she never had those captivating eyes or beautiful hair. At first, she was just a bunch of lines on a piece of paper. You're *already* a masterpiece, a Mona Lisa; you just *believe* the opposite. Cease listening to those around you who desire to keep you stuck in the same patterns to justify their fear-based desire to do the same; they only do this because misery loves company. Allow the love of the divine to define you; see the world through its eyes—live in its consciousness.

Just as the source is infinite; thus, never ends, neither does your process. Consciousness is perpetually expanding and evolving, and so are you! Forever in the process, anchored in God's *rest*; be still and listen to its voice echo in the deepest crevice of your chest.

Relationships

There are many kinds of relationships in our lives. Even though some may be more meaningful than others, our friends, family, work colleagues, teachers, and even our acquaintances play significant roles in our journey. On the most fundamental level of reality—there are no others; everyone is a projection of our energy. The entire physical realm we behold, *out there,* is the workings of our consciousness crystallised into form.

"The world is yourself pushed out. Ask yourself what you want and then give it to yourself. Do not question how it will come about; just go your way knowing that the evidence of what you have done must appear, and it will."
– Neville Goddard

Fundamentally, there is only one soul in existence, yet that soul, even though it may *appear* to have divided itself into many, hasn't really. Creation is an illusion in this respect because all are still one, even though everyone seems to be separate from each other.

When you harm another, you hurt yourself. When you love another, you love yourself. The best way to help yourself is to be of service to others; this is why each of us are born with certain gifts, talents and abilities. We must utilise them to help our society become aware of its innate oneness with the source.

In a close relationship with a lover, family member or a friend, for example, they'll often reflect the workings of our unconscious at us. When we believe something to be true about ourselves, the mind has a habit of projecting those beliefs onto those around us.

If you have limiting beliefs hijacking your perception, then you'll see those beliefs in the people around you. Through synchronicity and the experiences with those you're projecting onto, you'll see clear reflections of the unconscious perceptions to enable you to change them. This process only applies, however, if you're willing, to be honest with yourself and work *with* the reflections. People who take responsibility for their state of being live happier lives because they're living consciously. Consciousness, or to be *conscious* is the first step to freedom.

Any resentment you feel towards another comes back to you in the outer world. If you don't wish for a certain person to find true happiness, for example, they may not, and neither will you by holding onto such bitterness. We must *believe* in others and project onto them the divine qualities we see in ourselves. Everyone can be happy, wealthy, successful and at peace in this world. If only some of those who had enough money to last them a hundred lifetimes shared just a sliver of their resources, we could eradicate poverty around the globe within a generation! Humanity is a giant organism, and if everyone followed their true passions, we'd click together, resembling the pieces of a jigsaw puzzle. Therefore, we need to lead by *example* and follow the calling that echoes out our hearts; to show others that they can do the same.

The most important relationship is the one you have with yourself, because if you don't love yourself, then you can't truly love another. You won't be capable of seeing the best in others if you don't see it in yourself, first.

Many get into relationships out of desperation. As a result of the desperate vibration, they're emitting out into the universe, they attract someone equally as desperate. If you're single, learn how to be at peace within yourself, enjoy your own company, and believe that life will bring the right person to you when you're ready to *receive* the reflection they'll give you. Trust in divine timing, because forcing things to happen out of fear usually leads you down a primrose path of contrast. When you do this, you won't attract someone who is desperate or has ulterior motives of using you to avoid being alone, because you won't either. Quite often, you don't attract what you want; you attract what you *are*.

If you attract what you are, then be the person you'd like to attract! It's that simple, don't be desperate; learn how to *enjoy* your own company. Solitude is golden because, paradoxically, it's only when we're alone, do we realise that we're never alone, but one with the infinite consciousness.

The experience of using another to avoid being alone can be useful if you're willing to learn from it. If you're in a relationship and know that you fear loneliness, then investigate your perception. Bring into awareness, the beliefs that dilute your God-given power. It's time for people to own themselves, by first, accepting themselves as they are. You only fear loneliness because you don't love yourself, but why don't you? What's wrong with you? Why do you only see what's wrong? What about what's right? Man's beauty doesn't lie in his perfections, but his imperfections, because it's through them does he have reason to grow even more beautiful than he already is; even the rose has thorns.

When we love ourselves, we can't possibly harm another, because everyone reflects our self-love when we embrace who we are. Christ said love thy neighbour as thyself for this reason; thy neighbour *is* yourself, and I don't just mean those living next door to you, but everyone in creation has the same consciousness. Consciousness is the fabric of existence; consciousness *is* God.

RELIGION

What's typically known as religion today, to me, isn't real religion. The etymological root of the word religion is the Latin word *religare*, which means to bind. Contrary to popular belief, this doesn't mean to control the masses through fear and manipulation, but to realise one's innate wholeness of being. Back in ancient times, people would perform religious practices such as meditation and prayer to merge with their higher self. Any system of thought or tradition that doesn't help one achieve this binding through its practices, to me, at least, isn't a true religion.

The higher self is ultimately what religion is pointing one toward as it's the aspect of your being that's aware of the divine plan. When one heeds the guidance from their higher self, life becomes effortless, love reigns supreme in the temple of their being.

If you're Christian, for example, Christ is your higher self, if you're Hindu, it's Krishna, Shiva or some other Hindu God or Goddess, if you're Buddhist then Buddha is, if you're Muslim, it's Prophet Mohammed. When one buys into a set of religious beliefs, their higher self wears a mask of the being to whom they give their heartfelt devotion. Binding the physical mind to the higher self occurs when people cease *externalising* inner truths and awaken to the divine presence within themselves.

All things can be used for good or ill, as they are neutral depending upon how one uses them. The Bible has brought great peace, inspiration, and joy to many sincere God-seeking souls, but has also been used to justify all sorts of evils. This misuse of the scripture includes the genocide on the Native Americans by the Europeans when they colonised North and South America. In the name of Christ, they seized the land, robbed their gold, and destroyed their culture, slaughtering millions of innocent people in the process. The Inquisition also saw many accused of being witches and heretics burned at the stake simply because they used medicinal herbs from the forest to heal people, even though Jesus taught that the heart of the law is mercy.

At one point, St Teresa of Avila was accused of witchcraft, as her writings were too deep for the people of her time to comprehend. Many wanted her burned at the stake as her documented internal experiences made no sense to their external image of Christ—which was fuelled by the belief that they needed someone else to live their life for them.

"Blessed are the merciful: for they shall obtain mercy."
– Matthew 5:7

Conversely, many devout Christians *have* merged with the source through the sincere practise of Christ's teachings. There have been saints in every religion, but when one awakens, they see the truth in their own faith in others too. People, who proclaim their religion has exclusive dominion over truth are being hijacked by limiting beliefs, because how can you place limitations on an infinite source?

I grew up in a Catholic society. The Catholic Church has nothing against other faiths, and even recently Pope Francis has been on video saying that we're all children of God, regardless of our race, creed or religious beliefs. Of course, every religion is a mixed bag. The priests and ministers who claim their faith is the one true religion don't understand it correctly. The late Pope, John Paul II has even been photographed holding the Hindu scripture, the Bhagavad Gita. Most religious leaders promote world peace and unity, regardless of our beliefs. It's just those of a lesser understanding who see themselves as separate from everyone else. The dogmas within their religion, which separate by design, are hijacking their perception.

"God has no religion."

– Mahatma Gandhi

Christ, Krishna, Buddha, Guru Nanak, Lao Tzu; one thing these luminous beings all have in common is they embodied the same state of consciousness. I personally don't believe Jesus Christ wanted people to follow him in a religious context. He didn't come to the earth to create Christians but awaken others to their own Christ consciousness. Spiritual masters come to Earth to lead by example, to inspire us to germinate the *mustard seed* of the infinite within our souls.

"But as many as received him, to them gave he power to become the sons of God, even to them that believe on his name."
– John 1:12

Most religious traditions are plagued by dogma. These days, fewer people with a religious temperament are being born; most prefer a more scientific or new-age approach. Quantum physics, in my opinion, is merging science and spirituality, and I feel that over the next century or so, the systems known as religion today will become less prominent in our society. Figures such as Jesus, Mother Mary, or Krishna, won't be looked upon as Gods who we should get on our knees and worship, but symbols of our higher self, which ironically, is all they *intended* to be in the first place!

However, I encourage people to stick to what works for them. Maybe being religious in a conventional sense suits you, perhaps it doesn't; just follow the divine call in your heart because it's the compass needle that takes you to where you need to go. If you want to follow Krishna and chant his name every day, then go right ahead. If you prefer to follow Christ and serve the less fortunate in his name, then do so. Despite their limitations, religions that teach love, compassion, and unite the people regardless of race or creed can be of benefit depending on the individual's approach to them. Love is my religion; peace is my guide; surrender is my philosophy and faith is my fortress.

All religions have an exoteric and esoteric side. Exoteric being that which is generally understood, while the esoteric being the knowledge known only by a handful of people. Even though the exoteric, more conventional side of religion does have a place in this world, your faith begins to get real when you practice the esoteric side of it; to *experience* the divine within yourself.

The quarrelling between those of different religions is kind of primitive when you think about it. If people understood the true nature of physical reality, there'd be no dispute. Life is *subjective*; in a sense, we're each in our universe. What's normal for one person may be entirely bonkers for the next; it's just the way things are. Many religious wars have taken place because of this; countless groups believing they hold exclusive dominion over the truth, hoping to *crush* anyone who disagrees with them.

Cognitive dissonance is spawned by limiting beliefs that go against one's freedom to choose what they prefer in their reality. What do limiting beliefs do? They compartmentalise, inflict limitations and separation. The fundamental basis of the religions, the original teachings from the masters aren't the problem; it's the dogmas added to them as a result of people *misinterpreting* them. If you follow a religion, discard any ideas that convince you to condemn others for not believing the same way you do. Take what resonates and throw the rest away.

If we're to unite the collective, then humanity has to drop this cognitive dissonance. People need to allow others to believe what they prefer, regardless of whether their ideas agree with their own or not. Once not only the individual but the collective finally understands that physical reality is, indeed, *subjective*, we'll witness peace spread like wildfire around the world. The only thing that separates us is our beliefs.

Renunciation

In many eastern cultures, people believe that renunciation of all worldly possessions is a *shortcut* to liberation. Countless seekers throughout the ages have quit their jobs, left their families, and gave up all their possessions believing by doing so, they'll attain freedom from their mental turmoil. These people are motivated in such ways because they think that it's what they do externally that matters; that if they get the outside right, then the inside will fall into place. The truth is, however, that the outside only falls into place when we change our state of being.

"Many years still remain during which you must conscientiously fulfil your family, business, civic, and spiritual duties. A sweet new breath of divine hope will penetrate the arid hearts of worldly men. From your balanced life, they will understand that liberation is dependent on inner, rather than outer, renunciations."

– Mahavatar Babaji, Autobiography of a Yogi

Let's *redefine* the concept of renunciation, as the only thing people need to renounce is the limiting beliefs that form the basis of their old self. When a person lets go of the unconscious perceptions that are motivating them in ways that aren't aligned with their truth, their behaviour changes for the better. After adopting positive beliefs and faith in the support of the divine, people become motivated to act out of joy instead of fear. Ultimately, it's only fear-based beliefs that convinces a man to behave in ways that aren't true for him.

"In the end, only three things matter; how much you loved, how gently you lived and how gracefully you let go of things not meant for you."

– Buddha

The people I mentioned at the start of the chapter gave up their material possessions to become nonattached to physical reality—their goal was to transcend the inclination of allowing transitory circumstances to define them. Nonattachment can't be realised in this manner; however, they have it backwards. We can be in the world *without* allowing the forever fleeting scenes of the cosmic drama to define us. We don't need to escape from the material world to find inner peace, even though solitude at times is no doubt a requirement for people to realign. These are just limiting beliefs that convince people the material world is evil and that they're not supposed to enjoy the life that's been bestowed upon them by the divine.

The only way to realise nonattachment is to access the stillness in the core of your being. Once you experience this core, you automatically detach from whatever is going on around you. In this state, you become the non-doer as you watch the divine work *through* you.

This realisation begins the process of unravelling the layers of falsity cocooned around the core of your consciousness. It's most likely that, while your focus is on the present, you'll be pulled out of it by fear at times. When this happens, remind yourself that it's merely the old self doing all it can to survive by getting you to identify with it. The more you stay present, the more the illusions of the past burn in the fires of pure consciousness.

For years, perhaps, even decades, the old self has been what you *believed* was your identity, when you begin to identify with your inner self, it comes as a bit of a shock to the system. The old self does all it can to keep you identified with it, how? Through the fear-based beliefs in the storehouse of your unconscious. When fear pulls you out of your natural state, it's essential to observe and question the emotions to bring the beliefs into awareness. When you become aware of the ideas generating the fear, you'll be able to transcend their influence and embrace the here and now without resistance.

Healing is a *process*, and you must be patient with yourself. Some beliefs take a day to change; others may take years depending on how much momentum is behind them. Treat the process as a game because you're simply playing hide and seek with yourself.

Nonattachment is a *by-product* of this process. The more beliefs you integrate that convince you to identify with creation, the more you'll identify with the creator within. Paradoxically, by doing this, you'll begin to enjoy your life a lot more. Life will feel *effortless*; like you're riding a synchronistic rollercoaster of moment-to-moment awareness.

When one identifies with their core, they won't be attached to possessions, but this doesn't mean they won't own any. In this state, one is free to *play* with the world, and its experiences as nothing outside them can add or take away the wholeness they've realised.

My teacher, *Guru Ma, Ritu*, calls people who run away from the material world *escapists*, and I agree. If you need to sit in a cave to be disciplined, then you aren't. Liberate yourself *amidst* the fires of hell; because once you identify with your inner self while being subject to its flames, you'll understand what Krishna meant in the Gita when he said that *no* fires can burn it.

RESILIENCE

Resilience is an essential quality to have in life. Everyone faces challenges, in one way or another—we all get knocked down at some point by a challenging situation, a relapse into a negative pattern or an unexpected turn of events. However, it doesn't matter how many times we've fallen as long we get back up and push forward *one* time more!

The challenges of physical reality are aplenty, as the illusion of separation from the source and with each other are at its peak in this sphere of creation. Most people are hypnotised by the illusion of linearity and the belief that their physical body is all they are. Until they become conscious of their inner self, they live mostly through impulse, reactions and the fight or flight response.

Connecting with the nonphysical aspect of your consciousness, your higher self, can help you become more resilient whenever things don't go your way. The higher self is beyond linear time—it sees all the potential timelines your choices could take you before it and guides you via your intuition. There's a big picture to everything that happens in life. As I said in another chapter, something that happened to you a decade ago could end up serving you next week. So, when something your mind automatically *assumes* as dreadful happens, take a deep breath with the knowledge that all circumstances are transitory —this too shall pass.

Your definition of a situation largely determines what you get out of it. So, redefine your concept of challenges altogether, because obstacles are simply opportunities to reinforce the notion that you're a *victor* and not a victim to your creative power!

Resilience applies in all walks of life, whether you're a single parent, an elite athlete or a successful businessman, there are always going to be ups and downs. The best tennis players in the world, such as Novak Djokovic and Rafael Nadal, for example, have mastered the art of resilience. There have been many times when Nadal, especially has bounced back from injury to retain the world number 1 spot in the rankings. Many said that due to his physically demanding playing style that he'd have a shortened career, but he and Djokovic have recently just won their twentieth Grand Slam title. Novak and Rafa also often have the highest percentage of break backs immediately after they've lost their serve at the end of the season. They have trained themselves to put whatever happens in the previous point or game behind them and focus on the here and now, an ability that often gives them the psychological edge over the younger players, especially in five-set matches. Watching Nadal and Djokovic on the court is an excellent lesson for anyone who struggles with resilience; they're an inspiration to me and many others around the world.

Those in the process of integrating the beliefs that weigh them down will need to be resilient. Yes, we should be playful throughout the process as much as we're capable, but there are no doubt times when things have been taken seriously as well. There are going to be days when you feel so overwhelmed by the emotional resistance of the old self as you become more aware of it. Self-awareness usually *magnifies* the resistance when you shine the light of conscious awareness onto it. How you respond to these off-days says everything about you.

If there are habits you wish to overcome but find yourself succumbing to temptation all the time, then you need to be *motivated* correctly. Self-awareness is only the first step of transformation; you must also desire to change more than staying in the prickled nest of patterns that prevent you from realising your potential. You can be aware of a habit but still, find yourself indulging, and this is because you're unaware of the motivations *reinforcing* the behaviour.

Let me ask you a straightforward question; why do you believe staying in that pattern is more desirable than change?

During the process of changing habits, people usually fail many times before they've suffered enough to generate the desire to change, but is all this suffering necessary? Instead of trying to fight old patterns, why not develop behaviours that render them obsolete? You can create new habits within three weeks of consistent practice. Many make the mistake on the spiritual path of battling their shadow, which is an exhausting thing to do; however, this process doesn't need to be a battle, per se. Focus on building a new self, with new habits and behaviours and the synaptic connections in the brain of the old self will eventually begin to untangle and lose their momentum.

"Forget the past," Sri Yukteswar would console him. "The vanished lives of all men are dark with many shames. Human conduct is ever unreliable until anchored in the Divine. Everything in future will improve if you are making a spiritual effort now."

-Sri Yukteswar Giri: Autobiography of a Yogi

All you can do is your best. As long as you make an effort, then you've controlled the controllable; the source will take care of the rest in perfect timing. Stay light-hearted on the path, but also fierce and courageous whenever circumstances test your resolve. You and many others are in the process of cleansing the emotional body of humanity. Disempowering beliefs and mindsets are being churned out of the ocean of the collective consciousness; usually, the poison reveals itself before the nectar.

Your bouncebackability is crucial; how you respond to the falls determines whether you realise your destiny or not. So, keep going. Have faith in the bigger picture; your higher self has got you, and you've got this. Once you know, without any shadow of a doubt, that the cosmic composer in the source orchestrates your life, you'll *flow* with the outcomes that arise from the actions you take.

SELF-HATE

Why do people self-hate? There are a few factors, but the main reason is that they're buying into other people's opinions of themselves, and as a result, shun their true nature. They don't have to buy into these beliefs; though, they can take back their power and accept themselves as they are, *including* their blemishes. Each person on this planet is unique; just as no two snowflakes are the same, so too is every soul in existence a *unique* expression of the divine.

Humanity was created to click together, resembling the pieces of a jigsaw puzzle. Every piece is of *equal* value because if even one were missing, the picture would be incomplete; that's how valuable you are to the collective. The divine only creates masterpieces, but unfortunately, most play the role of victim when they believe the negativity society drills into their mind. As we move into a new decade and the frequency of the planet ascends to unprecedented levels, it's time to be who you know you are. When one accepts themselves, they fit into the big picture. Paradoxically, if one is lying to themselves so they can fit in with everyone else, they are only shutting themselves *out* from the collective.

When others are hateful toward you, it's because they hate themselves; only hurt people hurt others. Those who've yet to accept themselves often belittle others for their imperfections. If someone is resentful towards you, realise that they're hating themselves *through* the reflection you're giving them. It is no different than them being stood before a mirror and not being able to stand what they see. The most mature thing you can do is not to take it personally. Have compassion; they don't hate you, but themselves, because if they accepted who they are, they'd have no choice but to accept you too.

If you struggle with self-hate, ask yourself why? Do you believe others are perfect? Do you think you have to live to please everyone? Do you think you have to hide your true self to be accepted by those around you? Are you comparing yourself to others? We can't please everyone. Even Jesus, Krishna and Buddha had their haters. In this reality, there's always going to be some form of opposition aimed at you by others. These people serve to *test* you; it's all part of the divine plan. When you can be happy regardless of another's opinions of you, and not allow their projections to define you, then you've realised self-acceptance.

When it comes to comparing yourself to others, you need to understand that it's actually not possible. If all souls in existence are unique, how then, can you be compared to another? You can't compare two jigsaw pieces as they are different shapes, colours and sizes, yet, as I wrote before, they are equally *valid*, as the picture would be incomplete without either of them. Cease comparing yourself to others and accept your God-given individuality.

True love starts with *you*. You must fall in love with yourself, which includes owning your weaknesses, so you'll be capable of loving others as they are too. This reality resembles a hall of *mirrors*; every person we interact with reflects an aspect of ourselves at us. Once you've accepted yourself as you are, then you'll project that acceptance onto everyone around you. When you see yourself in all and love what you see, then, undoubtedly, the love of God has awakened in thee.

"Those who perceive Me (divine consciousness) everywhere and behold everything in Me, never lose sight of Me nor do I, lose sight of them."
– Bhagavad Gita 6:30

In a deeper sense, self-hate is an *illusion*. You only hate yourself because of the false beliefs in your unconscious, which simply aren't true. Rid yourself of these beliefs! Take back your power and accept yourself for the masterpiece that you are. You *can* be a work in progress and a masterpiece simultaneously, who says you can't? Society may, but what does this kind of society know? You must think for yourself to be happy and realign with the integrity of your soul. In doing this, you'll be a shining example unto all who are around you. The fire of self-love in your heart, will, eventually, ignite the love in others.

Don't get me wrong; it's fine to observe a pattern within you that you don't prefer and desire to change; but it would help if you didn't hate yourself for your shadow. We all make mistakes, and the contrast they give us enables us to align with *better* versions of ourselves.

Real progress occurs when you accept where you are in your process. It's normal to have fears and bad habits, and it's perfectly fine to make mistakes because we can never stop improving as people. Make all the darkness *valid* within you; when you accept both sides of the coin, you're capable of perceiving the true light of non-duality.

SPACE

Neuroscience has taken huge strides over the last few decades, especially with studies done on altered states of consciousness invoked by practices such as prayer and meditation. One thing the scientists have discovered is that focusing our awareness on the space around us slows down our brainwaves, which in turn brings the brain and body back into equilibrium.

Ever been stargazing? The stars always make me feel at peace, at ease, no matter what kind of day I've had and now I know why. When you enter your living room, what's the first thing you notice? Maybe the couch, the coffee table, the television, or the pictures on the wall—it's natural for us to focus on the objects we perceive with our senses, but what is it that allows those objects to be? What gives them a platform to exist? *Space! The final*—joking, let's continue!

Space isn't empty; it's brimming with energy and information that's around us at all times. *Nikola Tesla,* who is regarded as one of the greatest scientists of the last century, declared that space is filled with a primary substance, the essence of all things, which he labelled as prana or lifeforce energy. Atoms themselves are 99.999% space, and this space is ultimately consciousness—the fabric of existence.

Convergent focus vs Divergent focus

There are two ways to focus our awareness; a *convergent* focus is when we narrow our attention on the objects in the outer world or on a thought or emotion in our inner world. While in a narrow focus, we live in separation from our timeless self as the smokescreen of linear time clouds our perception. Conversely, a *divergent* focus is an opening up of one's awareness on the space around them, such as the room they're occupying, for example.

Neuroscientists have discovered that when we're living through stress response, we *focus* on the cause of what triggered us into survival (a convergent focus). Our brainwaves speed up into high-beta, and we get trapped in negative, fear-based thinking and feeling loops because we believe we're in danger. When one sits down amidst the turbulent emotions they feel and focus their attention on the space around their body and in the room around them (a divergent focus), they *slow* their brainwaves down. As a result, they change their state of being and move back into alignment with their inner calm.

In a nutshell, you can *change* your emotional state and switch off the stress response simply by focusing on the space around you.

Let's go stargazing again! As you gaze at those radiant spheres shimmering in the sky, you hone your awareness in on the space between you and the stars—this *slows* your brainwaves down. When you calm the electrical storm between your ears, you feel at peace, at ease within yourself. Stargazing changes your state of being and quells the stress response if you're truly present as you do it.

If during meditation one experiences, even if just for a few seconds, stillness, they're tapping into space within their bodies. When they focus on the space without, they also align with the space within. This is because the inner and outer worlds are fundamentally the same—stillness is space in the *inner* universe.

Learning how to broaden your focus and making the practice routine enables you to *maintain* the state of being you prefer throughout your day. Stillness is your essence, your core-self. Making an effort to connect to this essence daily is the key to discovering joy, peace and happiness independent of outer circumstances.

"In the stillness of the mind, I saw myself as I am—unbound."
—Nisargadatta Maharaj

A consistent practice of meditation is essential in this day and age. Not only does it align us with the space within and around us, but it gives us a place to rest amidst the turbulence of everything happening in today's world. Meditation wraps us in a protective bubble, so situations don't bother us.

As we awaken more of our true selves, we become aware of the fear-based programs hijacking our consciousness. We also realise that our state of consciousness mirrors our perception of the world, and attune to the vast, cosmic intelligence all around us, effortlessly synchronising everything in the manifested universe.

Space and time are two sides of the same coin. In our natural state of alignment with our higher self, time feels non-existent; this is where the saying, *time flies when you're having fun*, comes from. As a creative person who writes and draws almost every day, when I'm in a creative flow, hours fly by; it's as if I skip over them without realising it. This only happens when I get beyond myself, allowing the intelligence of my higher self to work through my body, the instrument. In my true self, I am nothing, no person, but also, one with all that is. I *become* the space and, in the process, transcend time.

So, in conclusion, space aligns us with our very own portable paradise. Gaze into the horizon at the beach, watch the sunset or the stars—learn to consciously *switch* from a convergent to a divergent focus. Most do this without realising, but by making it a conscious practice by focusing on the space around you, you'll be able to *manage* your state of being, which can only lead to a more fulfilling and meaningful life.

STILLNESS

Stillness is *essential* to the meditative life. To be still is to raise your vibration to such an extent, that you become identified with your essence beyond form. Paradoxically, however, in that void is everything you need. To be still is to *commune* with the divine, as your soul is a wave upon its ocean of consciousness.

"Be still and know I am God."
– Psalm 46:10

In stillness, you transcend the distortions of the old self that generate all sorts of confusion and limitations for you. You're able to see the way out of the misery making *labyrinth* of your conditioning; this is why it's vital to introspect when you're in a relaxed state. You're able to see *more* of the baggage from the vantage point of a higher state of consciousness.

"Be still, stillness reveals the secrets of eternity."
– Lao Tzu

Stillness is the key to going beyond duality. When your mind defines a situation in a way that doesn't serve you, first and foremost, *accept* what's happening. Don't try to redefine the circumstance with the mind from a triggered state. Accept what is in that moment and then act *from* that acceptance. Once you embrace what the present moment contains, then the higher self automatically redefines the circumstance for you. It's only from a calm standpoint are you capable of perceiving what is, and not what was.

Lao Tzu said the universe surrenders to the mind that's *still* for this reason; the canvas of physical reality turns blank every time you embody stillness. He understood the neutrality of all circumstances and that we can change how we look at things once we still the winds of madness between our ears. When a challenging situation manifests in your life, retreat into your core and be still. The answers to your questions, the solutions to your challenges are *within* you. When you know how to access this portable paradise, you'll come to see just how inwardly free you already are.

Stillness is pure consciousness, your unconditioned self. Your core is the *kutastha chaitanya*; the level of your being that remains untouched by the dual-bound nature of physical reality. When you identify with this core, your life blossoms like a rose. You flow gracefully in the unknown, immersed in the still-waters of the present and behold how loved and supported you are by life. Miracles are everywhere if you have the eyes to see them.

Life always gives you what you need. You mostly attract what you *are*; even if you're being someone you're not, you align with situations to *highlight* your misalignment. These experiences still give you what you need, though, because if you're not honouring your true self, you need a wake-up call to show you.

One of the easiest ways to be still is to be *creative*. Whether you like to write, paint, draw or play the piano; muse and inspiration are given to us from the source if we're open to it. All great artistic expressions and works throughout history were brought into existence via the channelling state. You can't force creativity; however, it must flow naturally from the depths of your soul. In a sense, it will feel as if it's not you who is the doer; this is because it's not you as the ego creating, but the true self, which is ultimately, the source of all things.

"Actions that are performed for selfish gain are karmically binding. Therefore, Arjuna, perform your duty without attachment in a spirit of religious self-forgetfulness."

– Bhagavad Gita 3:9

People need to get out of their own way. The self they've identified with for so long is an *illusion*; it's simply a collaboration of their unconscious associations with timelines that no longer benefit them. Once you wipe your windows of perception *clean*, you'll perceive the light of your true self, unsoiled by the blemishes of the so-called past.

Be still and *feel* more; people overthink and hardly feel their emotions. Contrary to popular belief, stilling the mind isn't to force yourself to stop thinking; it doesn't work like that, as attempting to force anything in life is *resistance*. While meditating, keep a watchful eye on your thoughts; accept all you see—be the impartial witness. *Allow* the mind to go off on its usual tirade and eventually, you'll elevate your awareness beyond its automatic ramblings. When you transcend the thinking mind, it stops because you're not in resistance to it. The overactivity of the brain gets worse every time you resist a thought. Relaxation, razor-sharp awareness, and acceptance are the keys to stillness.

Your essence is *transcendent* of thought and emotion, but you often overlook it by identifying with them. After some practice of meditation, you'll always be aware of the deeper level of your being, even while experiencing thought and emotion. To be in the world but not off it is precisely this; with a foot in each world, you'll take this one by storm.

To be still is to trust; you must *let go* to be still, as the mind's automatic processes often resist life. The old self is continuously striving to figure out how things will unfold, brooding over memories, and buying into fear-based assumptions that reflect the illusions of the past. The spiritual path, the meditative journey, ultimately boils down to trusting in life and refining the mind, so it understands its purpose of being. When you embrace the present without resistance, peace, love, and creativity manifest effortlessly.

Surrendering to the nonlinear intelligence within your consciousness gets you to where you need to go. Only with a high degree of faith can you live a meditative life. Faith is generated by positive, expansive beliefs that, eventually, becomes *knowing* through the experiences it manifests. When you know your truth by actual realisation and not by blind faith alone, it becomes unshakable; thus, nothing that happens in the outer world can seize it from you. Be loyal to your *experiences*, not your beliefs.

Be still, be chill and align with God's will.

SYNCHRONICITY

Synchronicity is being experienced at an accelerating rate as more and more around the world awaken to their true selves. To me, synchronicity is proof of a higher order, a cosmic intelligence that oversees creation. When one observes their life with awareness, they see that all things, *beyond* appearances, are ultimately one.

The wonder of synchronicity has two forms, positive and negative, but even the negative become positive if you're willing to pay attention to what they are showing you. If there are fear-based beliefs in your unconscious that you've yet to bring into awareness, then you'll manifest wake-up calls to force you to face the ideas reflected by them. Almost everything we experience has its origin in our beliefs. Many create without awareness and at the same time, blame karma or fate for the so-called bad things that happen to them.

Working with this form of synchronicity is one of the keys to learning your lessons at an accelerated rate. *Listen* to the universe; it's always nudging you via the signs and situations that appear in your reality. Pay attention to them. Even your spirit-guides use synchronicity to push you back into alignment with the divine plan.

"Synchronicity is an ever-present reality for those who have eyes to see."

– Carl Jung

Positive synchronicities appear to show you that you're in harmony with existence. They manifest to encourage you to keep going in the same direction. These signs are your higher self telling you that you're on the right track and aligned with divine timing. Let's say, for example, you want to start playing the guitar, so you go out and buy one. A couple of days later, when you're least expecting it, you meet someone for the first time who plays the same instrument, and you become close friends—this is literally the universe telling you: *"Follow the breadcrumbs, it's where you need to go!"*

It is common for people in the beginning stages of the awakening process to start seeing numbers such as 11:11, 333, 777, 111, and 222. These signs are reminders that everything is connected, and that you're creating your life. As you probably know by now, everything in physical reality is neutral, so you can assign whatever meaning you prefer onto the numbers. I often see 21:12, and every time I see these numbers, I know the universe is telling me that I'm where I need to be. The experience is different for everyone, of course, maybe you don't see numbers, perhaps other signs remind you just how powerful of an impact your mind has on your reality.

The etymological root of the word synchronicity is the Greek, *Chronos*, who is the God of time. The definition of words such as synchronicity or synchronism is a coincidence in time; to me, however, there are *no* coincidences—the cosmic composer, our higher self, orchestrates our life from a nonlinear perspective. There's a big picture to everything that manifests; no matter how tumultuous the storms of life become. Trust in life, *allow* the higher self to guide you to the fulfilment of your soul's desires through synchronicity.

Follow the synchronicities that inspire you, as they are the yellow brick road that take you home to the Promised Land. When you have a desire and set an intention, you must let go of the mind's need to know *how* things will come about. Don't concern yourself with this; train yourself daily to let go and let God. When you successfully achieve the state and act when called upon, you'll behold a synchronistic bridge of incidents appear before you to lead you to the fulfilment of your desire.

"Signs follow, they do not precede."
– Neville Goddard

Never look for synchronicities, allow them to find you. Looking for signs keeps you stuck in a repetitive loop that prevents you from moving to the reality of your fulfilled desire. If you're on the lookout for signs, then you've yet to let go of the need to know *how* your wish will come about. Follow the yellow brick road by befriending the unknown. Allow your higher self to guide you to where you need to go, step by step, lane by lane; this is the art of living on the material plane.

God's ways are mysterious; they are not our own. The higher self can manifest things that the thinking mind isn't capable of imagining. Most attempts of trying to predict how things will happen in the future are in vain, don't even bother trying; it's a waste of your time and energy. Become comfortable in the state of not knowing, with a receptive mind, allow your intuition to be your one and only guide.

THE UNKNOWN

Most fear the unknown, or what is unfamiliar to them. As a result, they'd rather stay comfortable, in the known than experience something new. Once indulged in over an extended period, their self-sabotaging habits become their biggest addiction, but it's only fear that keeps them confined to them. If your patterns make you suffer daily, however, then they are anything *but* comfortable.

The only comfort zone that truly exists is to align with the higher self, but even that takes the courage to embrace what's *unfamiliar* to you; this is why you need faith. Faith is absolute trust in the direction life is taking you, to get out of your way and allow the source to work through you. Another aspect of faith is the knowledge that you can only discover more of yourself in the unknown. Allow faith to be your fortress and embrace your life.

People often experience reoccurring themes in their comfort zone. They manifest similar situations via the unconscious use of their creative power, which in turn triggers the fear-based emotions in their body. Feelings, however, as Goddard taught, are the *secret.* They are the key to creating with intention as they reflect our *conviction*. If you're feeling fear daily without questioning or working with it, then you'll continue manifesting circumstances to reinforce it.

So many are afraid to face themselves because they believe what society has told them must be true. Because of this, many sit on the fence, leaning towards the negative side of things. People are usually afraid to check their feelings to see if things they tell themselves are true, yet still, allow the fear to *define* them. As a result of this unconscious process, they identify solely through the eyes of other people. Let me tell you, however, nobody can define you unless you align with their perception of you.

Most people don't know who they are, so why do you believe they know who *you* are? It's simply not possible; man, only knows the world when he knows himself. Many of the things people project onto you aren't a representation of you, but a *reflection* of them. Physical reality is a hall of mirrors; almost everyone is reflecting our unconscious to us. Those who attempt to convince you that you're worthless, not good enough or undeserving of the beautiful things in life, only do because they believe the same about themselves.

Another paradox is that you'll never discover who you are until you give up the *need* to know who you are. Because, in a similar way that the mind isn't capable of understanding how things will come about, it's also incapable of putting you into a box or defining you in a way that *completes* you. True freedom comes when you only allow the source to define you and not the impressions of the undecided mind, as a limited entity cannot represent an infinite source of energy. This consciousness, this source, is your very being and is God itself.

When you give up the need to know who you are, then life *shows* you. Not through the stimuli of the five senses, but in the immortal strength innate to the depths of your soul. As you break the walls of Jericho (resistance) down and become vulnerable to life, you discover who you are. When the higher self takes the reins on the chariot of your being, life becomes a joyride of infinite possibilities. All the limitations you believed your past imposed upon you are wiped away within an instant of being one with the present moment and the unknown.

You cannot be present if you're unwilling to embrace the unknown, they go hand in hand. The present *is* the unknown; it's a state of total let go and trust in the way life unfolds. The river only flows one way; you can either resist it by attempting to swim against it or allow the current to guide you. When you go with the flow, it takes you where you need to go because you're no longer controlled by the old self that's hellbent on keeping you in the familiar. Synchronicity leads you to the fulfilment of your soul's desires, and in a detached state, you live in a moment-to-moment awareness.

It may be challenging initially to embrace a new set of feelings. Leaving the comfort zone, of course, is going to be difficult since your body is chemically addicted to wallowing in the same emotions. This is why it's common for people's fight or flight response to activate when an unfamiliar situation arises. They panic because they believe all that's unknown to them poses a threat to their survival. There is a threat in the unknown, not to your true self, but the old self, and this conditioned aspect of the mind *knows* this.

The old self knows it can't survive in the here and now because the moment you become present, it's disarmed, and the divine ego takes charge. The old self's greatest fear is death, that's why it fears the unknown. Nothing can kill who you really are in the unknown; however, as only illusions are capable of perishing. The conditioned ego is *contrast*, or in other words, the reflection of what you're not that's required to perceive what you are. Every time you embrace the unknown, you're slowly crucifying this false self, and every time you embrace the known, you're suppressing the true self. The choice is yours; as Christ put it; ye are either with me (the true self) or against me.

Do we ever grow while we're comfortable? Not really. The key is to become *comfortable* with feeling uncomfortable. Once the feeling stops bothering you it will go away. It takes a tremendous amount of pressure to create a diamond, and it takes just as much adversity to create a diamond out of you. Trust in the process, amidst the fires of hell; *shine* anyway.

VALIDATION

Living *through* the eyes of others has become so prevalent in our society that most don't realise they're doing it. Much of the suffering people impose upon themselves is because they seek out other's opinions to form the basis of their identity. People's perceptions, however, change all the time, which includes their impression of *you*. You make a mistake, they judge you for it, and as a result, you judge yourself. Conversely, if you do something which benefits them, their opinion of you improves; thus, you feel better about yourself.

I'm not saying we should blindly discredit the opinions of others; sometimes it's wise to listen and take on board their perspectives, as they can show us things, we may not see in ourselves, that's all well and good. But, for your self-worth to be *dependent* on people, who, in most cases, don't believe they're worthy themselves is to be a slave to society.

You don't need validation or approval from anyone. Even if the entire world goes against, disagrees, or tries to crush you, stand up for what you believe in, and stand up alone if you must. It's better to die in your truth than to live in another's. Krishna, in the Gita pointed this out when he said to his disciple, Arjuna:

"It is better to live your own destiny imperfectly than to live an imitation of somebody else's life with perfection."

– Bhagavad Gita 18:47

Integrity is the key to freedom because only your truth can set you free. It's also fine if your perception doesn't match that of those around you because the experience of physical reality is, for the most part, subjective. Having different perspectives doesn't make either of you wrong, as long as you're both being true to yourselves. All perspectives of the truth, however, do fit into the objective structure of the universe—if yours doesn't then it isn't truth.

Many who seek the validation of their beliefs by imposing them on others, do so with the hope they'll agree with their views to reinforce them in themselves. If you need others to agree with you, then you don't believe what you claim to, neither do you know what's true for you, yet. When you know your truth, no one or no-thing can shake you, nor will you enforce it on another, as you'll understand the *subjective* nature of physical reality.

Seeking your worth in others never works. It ultimately doesn't matter what anyone else thinks about you because true love starts with yourself. People need to learn how to accept themselves as they are while also accepting *where* they are in their process of ego refinement.

When you love yourself, you transcend the inclination of allowing other people's opinions to define you. Many allow such a thing to happen because they have no idea who they are, nor do they feel comfortable, not knowing. They cling to their past to form the basis of their old self, which is a fictional entity generated by the mind's unconscious reactions to the stimuli perceived through the senses.

The old self lives *through* others; it seeks validation through their approval. The soul needs nothing but the love of the divine to sustain it. There are two ways to be defined in this world; through the mind, or the source—it depends on what one identifies with in the moment. If they're seeking themselves in the old self, they'll allow the outer world to define them. When immersed in the still-waters of the present, in their divine ego with the soul in charge, they go *beyond* what they always defined as themselves and become pure consciousness. In this state, one becomes a conduit for the wisdom of the universe. The greatest of all paradoxes is that in the true self, there is no set personality; you become fluid, malleable; whatever life calls you to be.

In the I AM of pure awareness; you allow the ego to focus your consciousness in the present while being guided by the higher self. You are what you are in the moment—nothing else matters. Many don't know how to access this state, and because of this, seek experiences in the transitory world in an attempt to fill the imaginary void they feel within themselves. When they stop seeking outside, they realise that what they were looking for was inside them all along, hiding within the shell of society's lies cocooned around their consciousness.

In the true self, there's love, joy, and peace independent of outer circumstances, and this is your natural state. In the pure consciousness of the soul, you're free from the inclination of allowing creation to define you. Only in this state are you *whole* within yourself, as you're using the mind and higher self for the roles the divine intended. The need for validation comes from a deep-seated need to be loved and accepted, but you'll never allow others to love you if you don't love yourself *first*. You'll only sabotage your loving relationships by refusing to accept yourself as you are.

YOGA

Yoga is our natural state, and not solely the asanas many in the west believe it to be. Yoga is union with the divine—your true self. When you're in sync with your higher self, living without resistance in the present, then you're expressing your innate wholeness of being.

Yoga is the state of balance mentioned all throughout this book. When we're operating between heaven and Earth, or in other words, the mind and the higher self, the soul can express itself without obstruction. What prevents the true self from expressing itself? The illusory beliefs of the old self.

I say *illusory* because every limiting belief is, on some level, a deception, as they persuade you that you're someone or something you're not, convincing you to sabotage your potential. Fear-based beliefs generate false thoughts and feelings that motivate you to chase things that aren't in your best interest.

In the yogic state, there is no old self, only pure consciousness, but contrary to popular belief, you're not required to stay in this state all day, every day. One, the feat is impossible; two, if you did, you'd get nothing done. Don't be *too* spiritual, as the desire to be thoughtless all day does nothing but create lazy people. We're here to find a balance between heaven and Earth; dive into the silence from time to time to draw clarity, wisdom and inspiration from the source, but also play the role as a person to the best of your ability.

Gain *clarity* on what truly matters to your human self and put your heart and soul into it. When you get clarity, you'll be inspired to go in the direction of your true passion, even if the prospect seems scary. Sometimes, we're called to do what doesn't come natural to us, which means we must *develop* specific skill sets in order to achieve our dreams. Don't be afraid to suck at something while you're in the process of learning, as a closed mind doesn't get anywhere.

Living in harmony with existence is the by-product of using the ego for the role it was designed rather than allowing its whimsical conditioning to control you. When you're using the ego properly, with consciousness, then you find yourself, in Biblical terms, in the state of *rest*. The state is *a rest unto your soul* because it fills your being with energy every time you enter it. People wear themselves out when they do too much with their ego by attempting to control every aspect of their lives. Renounce the throne of your being and allow the higher self to take care of the subjects in your kingdom. Christ referred to the state of rest when he said to his disciples:

"Take my yoke upon you and learn of me; for I am meek and lowly in heart: and ye shall find rest unto your souls."

– Matthew 11:29

The yoke of Christ is the yogic state of balance. The Sanskrit root of the word yoga is *yuj*, which means to unite, to yoke or bind. Coincidentally, it has the same definition of the Latin root for the word religion; *religare*, which also means to bind. My point is that true religion is *yoga*, and not the watered-down traditions prevalent today.

Yoga is the kingdom of God Christ said is *within* you. To be immersed in the bliss of the soul, however, you must, first and foremost, trust in life by having an unshakable faith in the way it unfolds.

The truth is simple; you're either aligned or misaligned. Everyone oscillates between alignment and misalignment; this is a common aspect of the process as it enables one to *progressively* peel away the layers of falsehood cocooned around their core. Trust in the process; all is well.

People would experience more effortlessness if they practised the art of staying present, but it shouldn't be forced. I mean, of course, there are times when it's good to stop what you're doing and focus on the breath to centre yourself. Being still is effortless when you do what sets your soul ablaze. It's important to follow your *true* passions and not those of another. Having the discernment to see the motivations beneath your choices helps you know why you do the things you do daily. The key to wisdom is to know yourself.

There is no fear in the true self, as it sees the big picture in every situation. The analytical mind is programmed to resist this; it wants to be in control of its reality due to its fear of the unknown and does all it can to remain in power. This book is centred on *rewiring* the nodes in the maze of your mind for this reason.

Rewiring the nodes in the maze of your mind dissolves resistance, thus, *allows* you to live in harmony with existence; this is the essence of surrender, which means to trust that level of your being that knows how and why things happen. The ego must have faith; it needs to believe the source supports it in everything that it chooses.

"Trust in the LORD with all thine heart; and lean not unto thine own understanding."
– *Proverbs 3:5*

The yogic state *burns* the misaligned elements in you. In this process, it's common for waves of the residual baggage to drag you back into fear-based emotions. This experience is a valid part of the process. There's always more to learn, to discover and realise, so don't define these moments as steps backwards, because they only become so if you do. If you're willing to work *with* the contrast, then you'll progress at an accelerated rate. If you suppress your fear, then it will only keep coming back, and most likely, stronger every time.

"Once you reach the top of the mountain, keep climbing."

– *Zen proverb*

The past is *contrast*; the present moment is the portal to alignment, and nowhere else. The yogic state is only accessible when you're willing to courageously dive headfirst into the unknown to discover the parts of yourself you've yet to find. If you've merged with the higher self, every time you jump off the cliff of your familiar patterns, feelings and beliefs, you'll be caught by the loving support of the divine through the synchronicity that manifests.

There are many names for this state, Zen, Christ consciousness, Yoga, Buddha Nature, and so on. These labels give people a point of reference. Some have also symbolised the state with iconic religious figures with the sun behind their head representing enlightenment. This light is who you truly are. There's nothing to attain, as the integration process is simply the reassembling of your energy that's been compartmentalised by fear-based perceptions.

"You don't need to aspire for or get any new state. Get rid of your present thoughts, that is all."
– *Ramana Maharshi*

Ramana Maharshi reiterates my point in the passage above. When you feel weighed down or misaligned, immerse yourself in your essence. If the resistance is too strong, then question the emotions in a curious state to bring the unconscious perceptions into consciousness. Resistance equates to refusing to agree with the divine about who you are, but the source *became* you—it knows you better than you know yourself.

"By constantly keeping one's attention on the source, the ego is dissolved in that source like a salt doll in the sea."

– *Ramana Maharashi*

The paradox is that you discover your true self when you're willing to go *beyond* the personality you believed was your identity.

"He that findeth his life shall lose it: and he that loseth his life for my sake shall find it."
– *Matthew 10:39*

Christ was a *Yogi*. His teachings parallel all the other Ascended Masters. He lived in the present, allowed love to guide him, and trusted in the divine plan for his life. Jesus surrendered to the will of God; in fact, there was no Jesus left, for Jesus was his persona; the son of *man* to which he often referred. He identified himself as the Son of God; the *Christ,* as he'd realised his innate freedom. The yogic state is the truth that shall set you free. This is also why Krishna told his disciple Arjuna, in the Gita to *be thou a yogi!*

CONCLUSION

I wrote this book to remind you of your true nature. There's nothing in it that your higher self doesn't already know. The sections that you resonate with are your own to put into practice at whatever rate you feel comfortable.

I encourage you to *lighten up* and see this process as a game you're playing with your old self—it need not be taken as seriously as people believe. Again, I reiterate, to go at whatever pace you're comfortable. If you prefer to investigate your perception once a week, once a month or every six months; it's important to honour where you are in your process. Enjoy periods in solitude from time to time because it's only in the silence do you hear the divine voice.

When you embrace the present moment as it is, and allow your higher self to orchestrate your life, it becomes effortless. Don't get me wrong; I'm not saying we should avoid activity and sit around all day waiting for the higher self to bring things to us; that would be *counterproductive*. What I'm saying is, the higher self will bring you outcomes you need as you immerse yourself in passionate activity. You can set positive intentions, believe good things, do visualisations, and embody the state of your preferred reality all you want, but if healthy habits and productive actions don't match all that inner work, then it will be in vain. I encourage you to act, as life responds to you when you align with your passion by acting on it.

Trust in your process is an *essential* aspect of the art of living. I also encourage you to trust how your life is unfolding, and from that trust and acceptance, act appropriately towards what the present moment contains. To live *without* resistance is to be led by faith, rather than the anxiety fear-based beliefs generate.

"There is no right or wrong path. There is only the path that you choose. Whatever you choose, there will be many opportunities for you to grow and expand."
– *Quan Yin*

All things can be used for your benefit if you tweak your perspective of them. Your choices either reinforce your joy or present you with more contrast. When you adopt this kind of approach and use all experiences as opportunities to expand your consciousness, they transform *into* blessings. The stars can only shine at their brightest when they are surrounded by darkness, and if used in this manner, your dark days can enhance your perception in ways you never thought possible.

Quite a bit of this book focuses on our beliefs because most of the things we believe about ourselves are not true; the word *lie* is in believe for a reason. Yet, these things feel so real because the outer world mirrors our perception. When you embody positive beliefs, you're aligned, as faith pulls the synchronicities and experiences that reflect your optimism.

Faith turns into knowing when you experience the *result* of it. When your faith attracts experiences aligned with the positivity you're putting out; then you know your truth through *experience*. I've left it to the conclusion to make this point for a specific reason; you won't even need to believe when you know what is true for you because your behaviour will reflect your knowing. Only when your behaviour aligns with your truth have you realised freedom; knowing and doing are synonymous.

Only through experience do you transcend blind belief and realise the truth for yourself—transmuting fear-based beliefs accelerates this process. When you *know* something to be true, then you do it regularly. You transcend intellectual understanding; it becomes second nature. When your behaviour reflects your integrity, you're breaking free from the fear-based worldview of the collective unconscious.

Knowing *transcends* the need to believe. Allow your faith to become so strong that you can even take it for granted that your heart's desires will come to fruition when the time is ripe. When your faith becomes unshakeable, peace reigns supreme in the temple of your being. Like I stated many times in this book, understanding the roles of the mind and the higher self is essential. If people knew how to use their ego correctly, they'd be at peace, as peace is a by-product of being immersed in the present moment. The old self experiences death every time you become present. When you release your attachment to whom you've been told you should be, you experience what you *are*.

The time is upon us to take responsibility for our state of being. Nothing happens perchance or by coincidence. It's time to stop blaming other people for your misfortunes. Take a good honest look at yourself and own up to the illusions you've fallen for, because it's okay!

Contrary to popular belief, it's common to realise that you're buying into illusions unconsciously. Please, don't beat yourself up over it, and there's certainly no need to define yourself as a victim. Shed the victim mentality that's had our society in bondage since time immemorial. The more people around the world take responsibility for their state of being, the faster our civilisation will evolve. Only through our example, can we transform society and inspire those around us to do the same.

Thank you, for being you.

-Rei Rei

Enjoy the book?

Reinvent Yourself with Rei Rei
Discover your Innate Perfection

Visit my website
for more
transformational content!
www.reirei.co.uk

Also, buy this book on Amazon?
Don't forget to drop me an honest
review! I would very much
appreciate it!

CONTACT

Rei Rei

Websites: **www.reirei.co.uk**, **www.blueorcaworld.com**
Email: **reihayashi1986@gmail.com**
Facebook pages: **Rei Rei, Blue Orca World**
Instagram: **reirei86_, blueorca_**
Twitter: **@reirei1986_**

Guru Ma, Ritu

Instagram: **@discoverwellnessandpeace**
Website: **www.discoverwellnessandpeace.com**

Divine Scarlet

Instagram: **@divinescarlet1**
Website: **www.divinescarlet.com**

Dr Bruce H. Lipton PhD

Website: **www.brucelipton.com**

Gina Lake

Website: **www.radicalhappiness.com**

Ayako Sekino

Website: **www.sekinoayako.com**

Lynne McTaggart

Website: **www.lynnemctaggart.com**